Diana
Her Last Love

Diana
Her Last Love

Kate Snell

GRANADA
MEDIA

First published in 2000 by Granada Media
an imprint of André Deutsch Ltd
in association with
Granada Media Group
76 Dean Street
London W1V 5HA
www.vci.co.uk

A catalogue record for this book is available from the British Library

ISBN 0 233 99887 X

Typeset by Derek Doyle & Associates, Liverpool
Printed and bound in the UK by
Mackays of Chatham plc, Chatham, Kent

1 3 5 7 9 10 8 6 4 2

For Arthur and Margaret

Contents

Part Four: The Final Summer

FOREWORD

'Where were you when Kennedy was assassinated?'

The murder of the American President on 22 November 1963 was one of those seminal moments for a generation. Yet by and large it held most resonance for Americans themselves. Seventeen years later, the murder of former Beatle John Lennon on 8 December 1980 evoked similar questions and similar feelings of the 'end of an era'.

Yet nothing has quite succeeded in bringing the planet together in collective shock and grief as the tragic death, on 31 August 1997, of Diana, Princess of Wales.

Where were you when you heard the news of Princess Diana's death?

We knew who John Kennedy was. We already understood the genius of John Lennon. Their untimely deaths immortalized them but did not redefine them. Before the car crash in Paris, most people in the world had developed an opinion about Diana. Yet the moment they learned of her death, a process began in which the Princess was redefined. We had taken her for granted, and now she was gone.

After the shock came a new appreciation of her life, and a tremendous sorrow for the sadness surrounding much of her existence. We suddenly realized that we hardly knew her at all.

Inevitably and almost immediately, the conspiracy theorists ran amok. It was the Marilyn Monroe syndrome revisited and doubtless such fantasies will be regularly returned to over the years. Most people, however, do not want to dwell endlessly on the circumstances of Diana's death but rather want to know more about this fascinating character in life.

I never met Diana or made films about her whilst she was alive, but it was easy to become infused with the prevailing journalistic opinions. We all had better subjects to write about and document than a woman the industry widely regarded as 'flaky'. That has all changed for me in the last year.

Where was I when I heard the news? On my honeymoon, in a village in the middle of Indonesia, at about midday local time, when the sound of clamouring voices made all the visitors turn around. The locals were clustered around a tiny radio, on which an announcer was speaking in a language I don't understand. The only word we could pick out was 'Diana', repeated over and over again. 'What's going on?' we all wanted to know. 'Diana, she dead!' That was about as far as their English would stretch. We thought it must be some kind of mistake. As the day rolled on, everybody else was also picking up the news. It was extraordinary. Old women in the middle of rice fields were sobbing, at restaurants and bars everyone talked in numbed disbelief. This was the island of Bali, and everyone could remember when Diana visited for a holiday in August 1993. They felt, as did the rest of the world, that Diana belonged to them.

For the next week, the only 'comfort' was to watch every awful reminder of the tragedy on the BBC's World Service, on CNN and a dozen other satellite stations from different parts of the world. Throughout, I felt a journalistic pull that told me my duty was back in London, to 'help out'. But what could I have done? I could only have massaged my own sense of shock through working out the tragedy in a practical way. On my return to London I went straightaway to Kensington Palace to see the incredible floral tributes, and to experience the physical sensation of a shared loss.

As time went on, more books and films about Diana appeared. We all thought we understood who she was. Her death now seemed to be explained away.

In May 1999, I was asked to make a film about Diana for London Weekend Television. I was not convinced there could be anything left to say about her. During the months that followed I met many many people who had been extremely close to Diana at different times in her life, and slowly I began to see a very different woman to the one I had assumed I knew.

As time progressed not only did my fascination for Diana develop but my admiration, too. I felt I was beginning to understand what lay behind her façade, what drove her and what haunted her.

Some of her friends who had been kind enough to give up so much of their time for me during the film making suggested that I should record my perceptions in the form of a book as well. There were considerations, not always easy ones – the questions of perceived intrusiveness and the possible effect on Diana's sons, to name but two. However I concluded that on balance the book could reinterpret key events, and could eventually provide a picture of those final weeks, which in the end might help to set the record straight and lay to rest some of the myths that have sprung up around her death.

If you ask most people to sum up the key moments in Diana's life, it is likely that they will include her marriage to Charles, the birth of her sons, bulimia, self-mutilation, the divorce, feelings about Camilla Parker Bowles, lots of holidays, James Hewitt, landmines, being on the cover of magazines, Dodi and her tragic death. A life summed up in twelve instalments, many of them unhappy. The woman that emerges from the resulting picture sounds one-dimensional. I felt there must be more. And indeed there is, both in terms of events and in terms of who Diana really was.

The period in her life between 1992 and 1997 has not been explored nearly as much as the years when she was married to Charles, and so much has gone undetected. Secondly, the focus has been essentially on the stepping stones of her life, rather than the building blocks of her personality. She wasn't forever the shy princess, or the broken-hearted wife. Diana could laugh; indeed she had a wicked sense of humour, and she was also considerably more intelligent than many people have given her credit for – she could read and digest a complex medical volume or a serious religious work, just as easily as she could devour a book by Barbara Cartland or Danielle Steel.

Above all, perhaps, one begins to admire the fact that she was able to survive so much that life threw at her. From her naïve entry into a loveless marriage, which quickly pushed her into the well-documented bouts of bulimia and self-mutilation, she became the woman who took on the world's governments over the landmines issue. Where did that strength come from? I became inspired to find out how she navigated that rocky road from hurt girl to powerful woman campaigner.

It quickly becomes apparent as you study Diana, that she was driven by her need for love, just as some are driven by the wish to make money or to find enough food to stay alive. To Diana, love was as fundamental as food or money. There is no doubt that she was deeply in love with Charles. He was her first love and would always remain a pivotal figure in her life. But she knew that it wasn't to be, and she needed to be loved as well as to love. By the end what Charles and Diana had discovered was a mutual friendship, which had she lived would doubtless have matured further.

If you look more closely you discover that the love Diana was seeking was not a simple quest for love of the head over heels variety – it was much more complex than that. It had to include a man, a family, the feeling that she was loved for herself, and that she could maintain the love of the public; without all those elements, Diana was lost.

In this book, then, I seek to find out who Diana was, and how and why she searched for her version of love, and the impact that search had on her own inner strength and feelings of self-worth.

Because this book focuses largely on the period between 1992 and 1997, a considerable amount of attention is directed towards Diana's feelings for Dr Hasnat Khan, a Pakistani heart

surgeon working in London. After Charles, Khan was undoubtedly the most important love of Diana's life; not only for
himself but also for his large family who Diana grew to know
and love, and finally for the difference I believe he made to
Diana during her life. That is why their story is told here.

I have met Hasnat Khan, but I must emphasize that he has not
contributed directly to this publication. His part in Diana's life
has been related by sources close to him, confidantes of the
doctor and his family. This is not a 'kiss and tell' story. I understand and respect Dr Khan's reluctance to talk publicly about his
feelings for Diana. I doubt that he ever will, which is how Diana
would have wanted it; she said herself that he was one of the few
people in her life who had not betrayed her to the press.

I thank members of Dr Khan's family in Pakistan, who knew
and loved Diana, for sharing their recollections with me during
the two visits I made to that country, in 1999 and 2000. They
have helped me to walk the fine line between invasion of
privacy, and understanding certain events that were to fundamentally shape Diana's life and help us gain a unique insight
into her thoughts and feelings.

I also want to thank all of Diana's other close friends and
acquaintances who gave up so much of their time to speak to
me and to share their memories of Diana, the person – as
opposed to Diana, the Princess. In most cases people have given
up several days of their time to sift through their minds, their
diaries, drawers for newspaper cuttings, many times allowing
me to see personal treasures in order that I can better understand the woman Diana was.

It is said that you can understand a person through their
friends. If this is the case, then one can speak highly indeed of
Diana, who seems to have chosen her friends – diverse as they
are in personality, nationality and background – so well.

Diana pigeonholed her friends and, on the whole, she kept
them very separate. Through talking to them, each in their separate compartments, it is possible at least to find corroboration
of key parts of what was going on in Diana's mind during those

latter years, and more particularly over that final summer.

Some critics have suggested that towards the end of her life, Diana had 'lost the plot'; that she was sinking deeper into some kind of madness. I disagree. I believe that Diana still had a long way to go, but she was maturing in many ways, and had she lived she would have surprised us all with new strengths and fresh achievements.

One by one, individual friends of the Princess are now also putting pen to paper, writing their own books. In each case the process will cast further light on this extraordinary woman, which I believe is a good thing. I do not believe that gathering such information is a betrayal; rather it is giving us a collection of memories by which Diana can be remembered as an even more extraordinary person than the world ever knew.

KJS, April 2000

PROLOGUE

May 1997, Lahore, Pakistan

The dome of the Badshahi mosque is scorched red in the dying rays of the late afternoon sun, dazzling all who risk a glance towards it. As dusk overtakes day, the strained voices of the muezzins resonate across the rooftops, calling the faithful to prayer. All over the city the ritual begins once again, as thousands of devout Muslims drop to their knees, facing Mecca.

It is the height of summer in Lahore, once the centre of the Mogul Empire, now the cultural heart of Pakistan. As evening falls it is still well over a hundred degrees, and the air seems to ripple with humidity.

In the smartest suburb of this otherwise harsh and impoverished metropolis, a pair of huge wrought-iron gates are heaved open by two servants to reveal a pale yellow, three-storey colonial mansion. A compact Japanese car sweeps off the busy road onto the curved stone driveway. At the wheel is a Pakistani woman, sister of one of the country's top politicians who also happens to be one of the most famous sportsmen his country has produced.

The black Toyota Corolla draws to a halt outside the house, and the passenger door opens. A woman climbs out. She is wearing traditional Pakistani dress – a rich blue shalwar kameez. But her costume is the only thing that manages to blend in. Everything else about her appearance belongs to another place, a world away; she is very tall with blonde hair, and European.

Out in the street there is a frisson of activity; some sharp eyes have noticed the visitor. This is hardly surprising, as the woman undoubtedly possesses the most famous face in the world. But the visitor doesn't notice the turned heads; she has other things on her mind. She is nervous and feeling terribly alone. But she must control such feelings if her evening mission is to succeed. To watching eyes she appears calm, cool and relaxed.

She knows this could be the biggest gamble of her life. Even fifteen years spent often at odds with one of the world's greatest dynasties has not prepared her for what is about to take place.

On the other side of the thick wooden door of the house are eleven senior members of the family she has come to meet. To them it doesn't make any difference that she is a Princess; as far as they are concerned she is here on trial.

'Hello, I'm Diana,' she says as the door opens. One by one she is introduced to them, but she already knows their names, having done her homework well in advance.

Absent from the gathering is the man Diana loves. The man who has prompted this visit.

By now the sun has set, and with perfect timing a sudden power cut plunges everything around the city into darkness. This is a regular occurrence in Lahore, but it is not the most propitious start to such an important evening.

Normally the family will struggle through until electricity returns, but given the occasion, a boy is sent to the local market shop for candles. Strangely candles do not appear to be a regularly requested item in such circumstances, and it proves too dark for the shopkeeper to find out where he stored them. By the time the boy returns empty-handed, the family have moved out into the vast walled garden with their guest, where they all sit under eucalyptus, banana and jasmine trees on the lawn, their voices accompanied by the atonal cacophony of hundreds of cicadas. The servants have been dispensed with for the evening, and the children have been ordered to stay indoors, as this meeting is strictly for grown-ups.

As everyone attempts to make themselves comfortable in the hard but exquisitely carved chairs, an aunt serves tea from an English-style tea service. Above them, the children sneak furtive glances from behind the first-floor curtains, straining to see what's going on.

Out on the lawn, old family stories are recounted, as always at a gathering of the clan.

The Princess takes tea, but avoids eating anything. She enchants the whole family but she is focusing her efforts on the one woman she feels she must impress if she is to marry the man of her dreams. Diana knows how important it is to get the mother on her side; she has already won over most of the family and believes she has their tacit approval for the marriage.

Diana has been searching for love all her life; now she is finally within sight of realizing her dreams. If everything goes well tonight she might finally be able to persuade the man she loves to commit to her . . .

Part One
The Real Diana

To understand what took Diana to Pakistan in May 1997, and the ensuing events of the last summer, it is necessary to revisit the main chapters of her early life, and attempt to unlock Diana's personality, especially her need and search for love, which was so fundamental it drove everything she did.

1

'I am unwanted'

'Let's make a den in the woods!' pronounced the children's nanny. Diana Spencer's eyes lit up at the prospect. Immediately the little girl trotted off to the large farmhouse-style kitchen with its Aga cooking range, to seek out the cook and head housekeeper. She asked the grey-haired and matronly Mrs Smith for some plates, mugs, pans, and other bits and pieces before scuttling back to the Park House woods with her assorted collection of cutlery and crockery stashed in a wicker basket.

Her younger brother Charles saw the den as the perfect place to play Cowboys and Indians, with the imagined Wild-West atmosphere augmented by regular barbecues and camp-fires. Diana, on the other hand, took a more practical view; she wanted to make the den into a house.

Her former nanny Mary Clarke recalls the way that Diana took to the task in hand with real enthusiasm, and busied herself making it into the most perfect little home that could be imagined.

As a snapshot of Diana's childhood, it is a simplistic one, but from it emerges the sense that even at a very early age Diana dreamed of creating a happy home, which would come complete with a husband who loved her and, of course, a large family. These were themes which would recur again and again in later life.

* * *

Park House is a rather forlorn-looking Norfolk grey stone mansion situated on the Queen's twenty-thousand-acre estate at Sandringham. Although the drab exterior makes the house appear somehow small and squat, inside it's a different picture altogether; the ceilings are high, the rooms are spacious, and when Diana lived there, the house had ten bedrooms.

The nineteenth century mansion had been acquired by her mother's family. George V had granted the lease on the property to Diana's maternal grandfather Maurice, the 4th Baron Fermoy, a friend of his son, the Duke of York. Diana's own mother, Frances Burke Roche, grew up there.

Her father's family seat is Althorp House in Northamptonshire. The imposing estate reflects centuries of accumulated wealth, dating back to the fifteenth century when the Spencers' business was sheep trading. For hundreds of years members of the family had held privileged positions at court. Diana's own father served as equerry to both King George VI and the present Queen.

Diana's parents married at Westminster Abbey in June 1954, and after a brief spell at the Althorp estate they moved to Park House taking over the lease from Frances' parents. It was here, in what subsequently became her parents' bedroom, that Diana was born on 1 July 1961.

Her arrival was greeted with cheers and sunshine.

It was a classic, lazy English summer day, beautifully sunny and warm, with the grounds smelling of freshly mown grass. To complete the picture, the Sandringham cricket team were playing nearby on the local pitch.

Just as Diana came into the world there was an enormous roar and a spontaneous outburst of applause from outside the window. It was actually for the local traffic policeman, who had just scored a century for his team, but it seemed to bode well for the future Princess.

Descriptions of Diana's childhood make it sound idyllic, full of fun and laughter. There were long walks in the woods with the dogs; she was surrounded by beautiful countryside in which she could roam to her heart's content, and she had lots of friends over to stay whenever she was home from school.

There was a pool at the back of the house where she loved to swim and particularly to dive; something she became extremely skilled at.

She also enjoyed drama, and the acting lessons clearly rubbed off on the young Diana, as she would often surprise everyone by coming out with great flourishing statements that drew attention to herself.

But if her childhood is portrayed as golden and wholesome in the old-fashioned way, this was not the picture Diana carried with her into adult life, at least not as she was to relay it to a number of close friends.

In Diana's own mind, as she was to tell her confidants, it was actually an unhappy childhood, leaving her feeling lonely and emotionally marooned.

In September 1967, Diana's elder sisters Sarah and Jane went to boarding school at West Heath in Kent. Shortly afterwards, Diana's parents decided on a trial separation, and Frances left home. Since the eldest girls were away at the time, the impact fell heaviest on Diana and Charles.

According to Diana's close friends her mother's departure was a pivotal moment in her life.

When Frances walked out on her marriage, she initially took the children away from Park House to be with her in a flat in Cadogan Place in Chelsea, London. However, on their return home for Christmas in 1967, Diana's father, Johnnie Spencer, announced that he had arranged for the children to be placed in Silfield School in nearby King's Lynn, thus ensuring that they would stay with him at Park House.

Diana told several of her friends about two particularly enduring memories of that time. She said she could clearly recall the sound of her mother's footsteps crunching across the gravel driveway, as she sat watching and listening on the steps of Park House.

Diana remembered then watching as her mother packed her long evening dresses into the back of the car, before driving out of the gates and away from the marriage.

Later she told friends such as astrologer Debbie Frank how she would go back and sit on those same steps for years afterwards hoping her mother would return.

'I think that was an abiding memory for her, sitting on the steps watching her mother pack her clothes . . . It was an image that was extremely profound and poignant for Diana,' says Frank.

Of the four Spencer children, Diana appears to have been most affected. In part that was due to her impressionable age – she was only six, while her sisters Sarah and Jane were twelve and ten respectively, and brother Charles, at three, was too young to know what was happening. And of them all, Diana was by far the most sensitive and least self-assured. Earl Spencer acknowledged to Mary Clarke that Diana had been 'confused' ever since her parents' marriage had ended, and had fluctuated between being bright and happy one moment, and quiet and moody the next. It was a painful experience for her. Speaking to her friend Simone Simmons, she compared the feeling to 'a big black hole; very empty with nothing to fill it up'.

It was this single event and the feeling that she had been abandoned, which perhaps more than anything else helped to shape Diana into the person she became – the person on the inside as opposed to the person we all saw in public.

Her mother's departure later grew to represent a kind of betrayal of her childish innocent love. It seems to have sown the seeds for her subsequent incapacity to trust people, and created insecurity so great that no love could ever be enough to satisfy her self-doubts.

Another of her close confidants, Roberto Devorik, doubts

whether Diana ever really recovered emotionally from her parents' divorce. He is sure that this chapter was what 'marked her in life'. In his view, later problems which were never really so serious assumed an unnaturally large importance to her just 'because of that disrupted part of her life'.

Diana's family had disintegrated, and in part she blamed herself for the breakdown in her parents' relationship. She had heard somewhere along the line that before she was born her parents expressly hoped for a son and heir because there were already two daughters. Indeed, eighteen months before Diana was born her parents had lost a baby boy; he was just eleven hours old when he died, and had already been given the name John. In contrast no girls' names had been thought of when Diana was born; her parents had been so sure of having a boy. And when Diana was christened on 30 August 1961 she had no royal godparents, unlike her two sisters, Sarah, whose godmother was Queen Elizabeth The Queen Mother, and Jane, whose godfather was the Duke of Kent.

In later life, the notion of being 'the girl who was supposed to be a boy' assumed enormous significance in Diana's mind, and she was convinced she was a disappointment to both her parents.

'From the word go, there were these feelings that she hadn't quite made the grade,' remembers Debbie Frank.

Diana gave similar renditions of her childhood traumas to many of her adult friends. Her perceived deprivations were not just idle comments, but heartfelt and oft repeated pleading.

Lady Elsa Bowker, another close friend for many years, describes the regular occasions when Diana would go to see her for coffee. 'It was hard work, because I always had to reassure her; to tell her she was loved, and she looked at me with doubt in her eyes. I said, "You have the world at your feet." She said, "You call this the world at my feet? As a child I was unwanted because they wanted a boy. Oh, Elsa, I am unwanted, I am unwanted." Always that word, "I am unwanted". It was a terrible word to hear!'

According to Diana, her childhood years were filled with all the material gifts she could have wanted, but none of the love and attention she so craved.

When Diana's parents divorced, Johnnie Spencer won custody of the children, and weekends during school term were spent shuttling by train between Norfolk and Liverpool Street station in London to visit their mother. Diana always remembered her mother's tears during those brief visits.

The school holidays seemed equally grim. At these times, during countless train journeys between parents, Diana seemed reserved and pensive; her thoughts were often on the parent she had left behind. On leaving her father Diana would say, 'Poor Daddy, we've left him all by himself,' and similarly on leaving her mother she would say, 'Oh poor Mummy, she's on her own!'

This was in some way an indication of the emotions coursing through the young Diana. But it was also one of the first signs of her ability to manipulate, through learning to play one parent off against the other.

In 1972, when Diana was only eleven years old, she effectively lost contact with her mother after Frances and her second husband, Peter Shand Kydd, announced they were moving to a hill farm on the remote Isle of Seil off the west coast of Scotland.

Diana was emotionally adrift. Denied her own happy and unfragmented family in childhood, she escaped into a world of make-believe, a fairytale world in which everyone was good, everyone helped each other and everything ended happily.

Young Diana could be observed creating a surrogate family as a means of receiving love and giving her affection back in return. She kept a menagerie of soft toys which took up so much room in her bed there was precious little space left for her.

Her former nanny Mary Clarke could see how Diana took pains to position each of the stuffed animals in absolutely the correct place every time she went to bed, with absolutely no favouritism given to any one of them. 'They all had to take turns to be nearest her at night.' Diana even referred to these soft toys as 'my family'.

At one time, young Diana had a pet guinea pig called Peanuts who went everywhere with her. In later years Roberto Devorik was looking at one of Diana's photographs of herself as a child, in which she was clutching Peanuts close to her face. Devorik said to her that he didn't think she liked animals. Tellingly she replied, 'At that stage of my life I saw these animals as if they were my children, my family. I needed that belonging, I needed to be surrounded with things that could give me love, and that I could give love back to.'

The fantasy world that Diana was creating was augmented by romantic literature. She could often be found curled up with not one, but several Barbara Cartland novels strewn across the settee. Mary Clarke remembers how Diana would devour such books 'at a tremendous rate of knots'. Hers was an imagined world full of love and romance, but perhaps more importantly, a world in which the lovers would live 'happily ever after'.

Mary Clarke recalls being a little anxious the first time she met the nine-year-old Diana, as the future of her job rested on their first impressions of each other, but she remembers how struck she was by their conversation on that day.

Diana was now at boarding school and the holidays were about to start. Clarke's first duty had been to drive over to Riddlesworth Hall, about an hour's journey from Sandringham, pick Diana up and take her back home.

Diana was waiting as Mary drew up in the car. Beside her on the ground were her trunk and all the paraphernalia that the end of term usually brought. They loaded it all into the boot of the car, and together they went back into the school to pick up Peanuts, the guinea pig, before setting off for Park House. Riddlesworth Hall allowed their pupils to bring their pets with them if they wished, and Diana looked after her guinea pig with such devotion she even won the prize for best-cared-for-pet.

During the car ride back to Sandringham the two of them talked incessantly. Mary started with some general, safe subjects, so she could get to know her new charge better. She asked what subject Diana enjoyed most at school. Diana said biology was her favourite. But very soon Diana 'somehow in her rather adept way' began to change the conversation round from rabbits and reproduction to love and marriage. 'It was all to make her point, within even that first hour, of her views of love and marriage,' Mary says now, 'which I thought was extremely strange for a child so young.'

As the car journey progressed, Diana confided in the new nanny about her plans for when she grew up and got married herself.

'She said she would never ever marry unless she was in love and she was certain that the person loved her, because without love there might be divorce.'

Diana ended the conversation with the forceful declaration, 'I never want to be divorced.'

2

'I wanted to turn back!'

'It's really ironic that you are now marrying the one person in the land from whom there can never be divorce.' So wrote Mary Clarke in a letter to Diana shortly after her engagement to Prince Charles was officially announced on 24 February 1981.

'If you are absolutely sure that this is the man you love, then I wish you every happiness, and offer my congratulations.'

For a time during her engagement to Charles, Diana no doubt drew some comfort from the thoughts expressed in Mary's letter, and felt secure in the knowledge that her marriage to the future king surely could not end with the two of them parting. It was unthinkable.

Diana had long been convinced that she would end up marrying somebody terribly important. According to Diana her father would tell her when she was little that she was destined for great things. Also, had she not read in her romantic novels that somewhere out there was a man who would literally sweep her off her feet? These strong, twin images of destiny and romance were embedded somewhere in her psyche.

So when Prince Charles proposed to her on the evening of 6 February 1981 in the nursery of Windsor Castle, it seemed as though her search for the handsome prince she had dreamed about as a child was complete.

Diana was very much in love with Charles, and in her mind the marriage was her fairytale dream about to come true – the answer to her quest for a husband and a happy family. As a young woman who was after all still only nineteen years of age, and who had led a relatively sheltered life, she was very susceptible to such idealized childhood images of romance.

It was all the more crushing then to discover that Charles was already in love with someone else. Diana later told her friends that when she found out about Camilla she was devastated, stunned beyond belief.

Of course, anyone who read a newspaper knew that Camilla and Charles had been an 'item' at one time, and that Charles had had a number of other girlfriends over the years. Diana was as aware as anyone else that she wasn't the first girl in her Prince's life.

Charles had first got to know Camilla Shand, as she was then, in 1972, when he was in the Navy. It was not the first time romance had blossomed between their families. Camilla's great-grandmother was Alice Keppel, mistress of King Edward VII. Charles was not ready to settle down, and in July 1973 Camilla married Andrew Parker Bowles instead. Charles had lost the opportunity to make her his wife, but she became his confidante, and their relationship would resume in the late seventies.

In the early stages of *their* courtship, Diana had believed the Camilla matter could be handled, in the sense that once they were married, Camilla would no longer be an issue. She certainly felt that Camilla wouldn't be a hurdle to a happy marriage. Somehow, Diana believed, things would be all right.

But the discovery very early on that this would not be the case, that Camilla still occupied a very large part of Charles's heart, was unbearable to the young Diana.

On 29 July 1981 the entire country – and beyond – was caught up in a mood of excitement and happiness. The one person who wasn't, was the one whose special day it was supposed to be. As Lady Diana Spencer left Clarence House for St Paul's Cathedral on the start of her journey to become HRH The Princess of Wales, her own mood was as close to despair as it is possible to imagine.

She was later to recount her feelings about the wedding day to astrologer Penny Thornton, who she met five years into her marriage. Diana had phoned Penny out of the blue in March 1986, after hearing about her from her future sister-in-law, Sarah Ferguson, and over the next six years Penny would serve as Diana's personal astrologer and confidante.

The most poignant of their conversations concerned what had been going through Diana's head on the night before the wedding.

Early that evening, Prince Charles lit the first in a chain of a hundred and two celebratory bonfires in Hyde Park, following which a vast fireworks display lit up the London skyline for almost an hour.

Diana told Penny that Charles was not alone that evening; he was with Camilla. She said, 'He spent the night before the wedding with this woman!' Penny remembers the words exactly, because she wrote them down in a notebook soon afterwards. Although it isn't clear whether the facts support the claim, this is certainly the story that Diana told her astrologer, and it had clearly left a deep impact on her.

It wasn't the only reason Diana's mind dwelt on the day before the wedding. Earlier in the day, Charles had told Diana quite categorically that he did not love her. From the way Diana related it, Penny thinks that for Charles it was probably an important thing to get off his chest; that he could now go into the marriage believing everything was square with Diana, and that she understood the score. For Diana, however, no matter how it was put, the revelation was devastating; her dreams were in tatters.

So whilst on the day of the wedding the air was charged with infectious joy and pride, as well-wishers thronged the streets to watch the wedding procession, and millions tuned in across the world, Diana's own perception of the 'happy day' was dramatically different. She was actually heading down the aisle in the full knowledge that she was walking towards a man who did not love her.

As she made her way towards Charles, her hand on Lord Spencer's arm, she looked shy and apprehensive, but nobody could have guessed what was spinning around inside her head. As she told Penny Thornton, the thought running through her mind was, shall I stop? Shall I stop? 'Penny,' she said, 'I wanted to turn back!'

Penny Thornton observes, 'Diana's own propensity to feel rejected was enormous. She really didn't have the resources within herself to be able to ride out the emotional difficulties of the early part of her marriage. She simply wasn't strong enough to meet Charles on equal terms, or to generate a sense of detachment about the way things were.'

In her new life as a Princess she felt very misunderstood and very alone. There were few people she could turn to, and she felt as if she was living a complete lie. As wife to the future king, she was expected to carry on as if nothing was happening, when in fact her whole marriage was falling apart at the seams. To someone who both believed in love and needed love as Diana did, such a situation must have seemed intolerable, desperate and a travesty of all she lived for.

It was apparent there was a change in her just from the tone of the letters she was writing. 'The lightness was missing,' says Mary Clarke. Shortly after her marriage Diana had written to her former nanny expressing her condolence for the fact that Clarke's husband was about to go away to Uganda. Diana remarked how hopeless she would feel if *her* other half went away.

In another letter, six months into the marriage, she told Mary that she was considering learning to ride. This had been a standing joke between them ever since Diana had a riding accident as a child. The accident gave Diana a deep-seated fear of horses and she hadn't been near one since. Now here she was, telling Mary she might learn to ride; it was simply because she felt it could provide a rare opportunity to be alone with Charles.

The marriage to Charles was a catalyst for all the painful feelings from her childhood to re-emerge – her insecurity, her feelings of betrayal and isolation. His apparent disregard for her emotions appeared to make such feelings more intense, and at times they overwhelmed her.

Diana, though, wasn't about to keep her feelings bottled up. She wanted Charles to see her distress. Whilst on honeymoon at the Balmoral estate in Scotland, Diana had become pregnant with William, and during her first New Year within the Royal Family, according to the account she gave to Andrew Morton, she threw herself down the stairs at Sandringham. It was the first of a number of often-quoted suicide bids. Yet these were probably more to draw attention to herself than in any real attempt to commit suicide. However, the more she displayed her feelings, the more alienated Charles became. It meant that by trying to win him back she was actually pushing him even further away. It was a terrible vicious circle.

Her bulimia – the often written-about eating disorder that so many writers and journalists took as some kind of evidence that she was cracking up – was another cry for help. Even the night before the wedding Diana said she had a bout of bulimia, and by the honeymoon it was much worse. She was suffering four bouts a day. By October she was so thin her bones were showing through. She lost the ability to deal with day to day matters; she became emotionally numb. Denied the love she truly sought, food was a replacement for the main element missing in her life – just an attempt to fill herself up with anything to hand.

The birth of William on 21 June 1982, and Harry two years

later on 15 September 1984, did little to alleviate the overall disillusionment Diana felt.

Diana's need to belong to a family was equally important to her, and psychologically she had hoped to find a substitute family with the Royals. But the family environment Diana wanted could hardly have been further removed from life with the Windsors, caught in a structure that was largely determined by history and tradition. The Royal Family, in turn, saw Diana's role as one of duty to Queen and country, and they had no time for her tearful outbursts and her often-violent physical remonstrations.

In later years she was to tell her close friend Roberto Devorik about a recurring nightmare she had after the birth of Harry. Argentinian-born Devorik once used to own a fashion store with partners in Bond Street and had been called on to dress the Princess before her engagement to Charles. In later years they came to know each other through charity work including the AIDS Crisis Trust, and Roberto became a trusted confidant and someone Diana turned to for advice. She told Devorik she had dreamed that her husband was about to be crowned King and she crowned Queen. The coronation was taking place in Westminster Abbey, and husband and wife were sitting together facing the congregation and the world. The King's crown was brought and placed on Charles's head; it fitted perfectly. But when they came to Diana, her crown slipped down around her face and neck. She struggled with it but just couldn't get it off. She was blind and started to suffocate . . .

Her subconscious seemed to be telling her, in a particularly dramatic way, that she would not be able to remain wedded to the Royal Family, and that her future really lay elsewhere.

3

The Unthinkable Happens

The real-life expression of the fears that lay behind Diana's recurring nightmare were to be played out over the course of many years, and came to a head in 1992.

The first public awareness of difficulties in the marriage came in newspaper reports as early as 1985. The following year, Charles again returned to his old love, Camilla Parker Bowles, after several years apart, and Diana's eating disorder, bulimia nervosa, showed no signs of abating. The Royal couple continued their public duties, but in private they were soon leading separate lives.

In November 1986, Diana began taking riding lessons with a certain Major James Hewitt. In a reaction to Charles's behaviour and as a means of attracting some attention, Diana soon embarked on an affair with him.

The son of a Royal Marines officer, Hewitt was a cavalry captain in charge of the stables for the Household Division of his regiment, the Life Guards. From the moment Diana met Hewitt she controlled the relationship, as was to become the pattern for all but one of her close liaisons.

In the summer of 1987, Prince Charles spent more than a month at Balmoral Castle, while his wife stayed firmly put in London. The press calculated they had spent one day together in six weeks, and there was a great deal of media speculation about a possible rift.

By 1991, the whispers were getting louder; reports were beginning to appear that Diana and Charles spent vacations and official visits in separate rooms, and by their tenth wedding anniversary on 29 July 1991, Diana had already embarked on the series of taped recordings with tabloid reporter Andrew Morton that would form the core of his book *Diana, Her True Story*. Diana was determined that the truth be known about Charles's relationship with Camilla Parker Bowles.

Although there had been a succession of years filled with unhappiness, psychological traumas and marital infidelities, 1992 became a particularly notable year in Diana's life – a major turning point.

By now her five-year affair with James Hewitt was at an end. Hewitt's unit, the Life Guards, had been stationed in Kuwait following the invasion by Iraq. Some months after the liberation of Kuwait on 28 February 1991, Hewitt had returned to England, but their affair, which had remained secret for a surprising length of time, had been finally exposed in the press. Diana had effectively lost control of their relationship, and finally ended it. Years later Hewitt said Diana had simply stopped ringing him or taking his calls; there was no cut-off, and he had had no chance to say goodbye.

Then, on 29 March 1992, Diana's father, Earl Spencer, died in hospital from a heart attack at the age of sixty-eight.

The Wales's were on a skiing holiday at Lech in Austria at the time, and the news of his sudden death was a severe shock to the Princess.

Up to that point in her married life, Diana had felt merely lonely; now she realized she was truly alone. 'To Diana, her father had been like a kind of visa in her passport of life. Then suddenly one day he was not there anymore, and she had to start travelling on her own,' recalls Roberto Devorik.

It was now becoming very apparent to Royal-watchers that Diana was deeply miserable. The signs of a beleaguered Diana were clear to see in many photographs, in particular the iconoclastic pictures taken in February 1992 of the Princess sitting alone in front of the Taj Mahal in India. Three months later a pensive Diana, again alone, was photographed standing at the foot of the pyramids at Giza in Egypt.

The expressions captured on video and celluloid were being interpreted as symptoms of an unhappy marriage. Diana had undoubtedly manipulated the photo opportunities to project an image she hoped would create public sympathy for her, as in her view nobody knew quite how trapped she felt, or how loveless the relationship with Charles was.

They soon would, for June that year saw the publication of Andrew Morton's book, *Diana, Her True Story*, which portrayed Diana as the passive victim of a heartless Prince and his cold family.

Any lingering hopes in anyone's hearts that the Prince and Princess of Wales might like each other, let alone love each other, completely evaporated. The book stunned the world, and succeeded in alienating Diana still further from Charles, his family and the Establishment.

However, it also generated a huge amount of public support and sympathy for Diana. By contrast, Charles was being cast as a callous and unfaithful husband. Nobody knew at that stage the extent of Diana's own personal involvement with the Morton project.

When, on 9 December 1992, Charles and Diana agreed to separate, events had come full circle; the one thing she had wanted to avoid at all costs – a divorce – now seemed inevitable. Her childhood fears of betrayal and being abandoned were being played out for the second time in her life, this time in the full view of the public.

The woman who emerged from that year had struggled through a constant series of exhausting battles – internally and externally. Diana was very tired. She needed to find peace; she needed to reconcile herself and her relationship to the world.

For the next five years of her life, Diana's home was an apartment in Kensington Palace. It became her refuge after the final collapse of her loveless marriage.

4

Home Alone

Diana wakes on the stroke of seven. Morning is her favourite time of day because that is when everything comes to life. She looks out of her bedroom window; all is quiet, but in places she can see the stirrings of human activity outside the Palace. It is like a new beginning, and Diana has no difficulty getting out of bed. She throws on a T-shirt, a pair of leggings and some trainers, and slips out into Kensington Palace gardens for her early morning jog. It is a daily ritual she rarely misses, no matter what the weather. The repetitive motion gives her time to reflect on the day ahead.

Kensington Palace is on the western edge of London's magnificent Hyde Park. It is a vast complex of gloriously proportioned apartments, each with their own private courts and garden areas.

Returning to the Palace Diana has a quick coffee, which she drinks with her butler Paul Burrell, assuming he has arrived for work by then.

After coffee it's time to face the real world, and in particular the very real traffic jams that inevitably punctuate her drive down to the gym for her daily workout. She is a keep-fit fanatic, and visits a gym every day in her search for physical perfection and the desire to cultivate her outward appearance. She has to prove at least to herself that she is attractive.

Her extended health routine occupies a great part of days that would otherwise be empty.

By nine o'clock she is back at the Palace. The hairdresser from Daniel Galvin has already arrived and is waiting to give Diana her daily shampoo and blow-dry.

If she hasn't already done so, Diana calls up a couple of friends. She tells them, usually at some length, how she is feeling, what she is doing and what she will be doing later on.

The telephone has become her trusted friend and greatest ally. It is just as well she has no worries about the phone bill because her calls to friends will sometimes last for many hours. She finds it necessary to check in regularly with lots of different people.

Diana always likes to have music playing, and contrary to popular belief she is a great fan of the classics. This morning Tchaikovsky can be heard drifting through the apartment, which is on four floors with a roof terrace at the top for sunbathing. She has redecorated since Charles left. Now her home is feminine and looks lived in. It has lost its severity now that the carpets with their swirling pattern of Prince of Wales feathers have gone, to be replaced with her own choice of pastel shades. It is very cosy.

She makes her way to her 'little lounge', or personal sitting room. This is one of her favourite rooms in the apartment, and is crammed full of mementoes and knick-knacks, as well as hundreds of photographs of all the family. These are the people she can hold on to, they are there with her even when she is alone.

In one corner of the room – the 'Knowledge Corner,' as Diana calls it – are some glossy books piled up on a chair, but they are just for show. Then there are stacks and stacks of books about Jackie Kennedy, and a biography and videos about Audrey Hepburn. Most of the publications in the pile have been given to her by people who thought she would find them 'useful'. She keeps the ones she really enjoys reading by her bedside. Typically these are by authors such as Catherine Cookson and Danielle Steel, but by contrast there is a copy of the Koran from her trip to Pakistan two or three years before.

Everywhere around Diana's apartment inside Kensington Palace there are reminders from the past. All the stuffed toys, which she had so carefully arranged every night as a young girl, are now in her Palace bedroom. They sit on the bed or on the little chaise longue in front of the bed. They all have their place, and they each have a name. For them nothing has changed.

She moves to her desk by the window. The telephone is readily at hand, of course, and the blotter is standing by in case the ink on her letters runs wild. There is always a pile of correspondence to deal with, but this is no chore. Diana loves writing letters; it puts her in touch with people.

Today's letters finished, it is time to visit a therapist. This morning she is having a Thai massage. In recent years she has increasingly turned to new age medicine, as a source of strength in dealing with her insecurities. She has begun to explore all forms of alternative healing and medicine, believing that such treatments will provide a way of coping with her problems, which are both mental and physical.

Her treatments read like a lexicon of complementary medicine. Diana dabbles with osteopathy, reflexology, acupuncture, shiatsu, massage, colonic irrigation, aromatherapy, acupressure, Thai massage, energy healing, chiropractic, herbal medicine, homoeopathic medicine, cranial osteopathy, psychotherapy and hypnosis. These are just some of the treatments Diana has got involved with. She has even taken a fancy to having fossils strapped to her legs.

On top of all of this she also tries out special diets: macrobiotic and microbiotic. She goes on juice fasts, and after her breakup with Charles has been taking sleeping pills to knock her out in the evening and pep up pills to revive her the following morning.

Diana's friends describe her as being a great 'searcher', who is tremendously open to other ways of living. She doesn't want her life to run on some sort of railway line, but wants to see what else is out there, and how else life can be lived. In that sense she is also porous, and wants to soak up other people's attitudes and ideas.

However, Diana has become almost totally dependent on the attention of these health gurus, psychic counsellors and mystics. She sees each therapist as someone who has been designated to look after her and only her. It is her way not only of psychologically trying to come to terms with her internal pain and struggle, but through the pampering and the attentions of the therapists, getting herself some of the love that she so craves.

When she is in London, her treatments have begun to take up the majority of the week. Sometimes she sees four practitioners a day, and at times has two colonics a week.

In short Diana has become a therapy junkie. Years later Diana will

admit that despite the plethora of diverse attentions, she did not feel any
better. In truth the therapies were often cancelling each other out.

After lunch the letters she wrote earlier in the day are signed; then it
is time for the rest of the day's business. Diana moves to the informal
lounge where there is a meeting with journalists, followed by a visit from
charity representatives.

This is life as Diana lives it at Kensington Palace following her sep-
aration from Charles. She compares her life here to being shut in a
prison or a gilded cage; the little bird is surrounded by gold bars; it can
see the outside world, but all it can do is stare from its perch and long
for freedom. If she goes out of the 'gilded cage' she will be surrounded by
hundreds of photographers, but if she stays in she is by herself. The real-
ity is that if she wants to have the boys with her, she has no choice about
where she can live.

She is the most photographed woman in the world – no other celebrity
has ever had such a global impact. She is a phenomenon, and an icon
of the times; she has hundreds of millions of admirers and is surrounded
by cheering crowds wherever she goes and yet something is missing. At
the heart of her fame lies a paradox; that of a vulnerable insecure
woman who cannot believe she is liked, and who feels very lonely and
isolated.

Such feelings are heightened every time she returns home to her empty
palace apartment. She may have been to a celebrity gala or charity event
where thousands of people love her, but the reality is that she comes home
to a TV supper, and is left with the sense of not having anyone to talk to.

Kensington Palace is a vast place, containing many 'grace and
favour' apartments granted by the Queen to various members
of the Royal Family. It contains the London residences of
Princess Margaret, Princess Alice, Duchess of Gloucester, the
Duke and Duchess of Gloucester, and Prince and Princess
Michael of Kent. There are also many smaller apartments,
some of which are occupied by servants of the Crown; Lord
Robert and Lady Jane Fellowes, Diana's elder sister, used to
reside here when Lord Robert was private secretary to the
Queen. Diana had her own staff including a private secretary,

two assistant secretaries, a butler, a housekeeper, a dresser and a cook, though none of them lived at the Palace.

Roberto Devorik paints a picture of the Princess in her 'home' environment. 'What is more sad than to be sitting in your own home alone? That's the image of Diana I had for many years; sitting between beautiful paintings, great sofas, wonderful objets d'art. She was sitting on her own waiting for weekends to come in order to see the loves of her life, her children. It was very sad to see a woman with such adulation and with the world at her feet, who after six o'clock was sitting with her tray, her soup, her glass of water or wine, night after night, because it was either that or knocking on the door of a friend, or big galas.'

Diana's friends say her loneliness was palpable; it was something that attached itself to her. Her friend and astrologer Debbie Frank says, 'Diana absolutely yearned to be loved, she was very needy for love through all her life. She got it from many different sources. Obviously from her boys, and that was very constant, and from her friends and from the public. She felt so connected to the public; it really gave her something to feel that she could connect with ordinary people. But in personal terms, in terms of her relationships it was something she looked for all of her life.'

Roberto Devorik sums it up: 'Diana was interested in love because it was the only thing she could never grab. It was like seeing an expensive watch in a window, and thinking, "I want this watch." You dream, and you save money, and eventually you manage to buy it. But the moment you take it out of the window it no longer has the same value; the fascination has diminished. Diana never took the watch out of the window – that word called love. She couldn't reach it as she dreamed to reach it. And that's the reason she went into relationships like an elephant in a crystal cage; relationships that many of her friends were totally against. It was out of frustration, and the sense that she wanted to be desired, loved and needed, but she never got what she wanted.'

In the gilded cage that was Kensington Palace, where she felt unloved and isolated from the world, the telephone became one of her chief allies. It was her prime means of communicating with the outside world, and as the years progressed, Diana spent an increasingly large amount of time talking on it, and not just while she was inside the Palace. By means of assorted landline, mobile and satellite phones, in whatever part of the world she happened to be, Diana would give a running commentary on her life.

5

'Just call me Diana'

Simone, it's Diana, I'm in a meeting. It's three o'clock now and I'm in a meeting for another hour. All went very very well at lunch and I'll tell you when I finish my meeting here. Anyway, lots of love, bye.[1]

The answerphone clicked and beeped as the message ended on the machine in a block of flats off Sentinel Square in Hendon, north London.

Anyone visiting Sentinel Square is left with no remarkable impression. It's not the kind of piazza where you sit at open-air cafés drinking cappuccino as you might in Battersea village, or sit and admire a row of beautiful Georgian terraces as you would in Hampstead. Instead, youngsters swing on the lamp-posts in front of Tesco's supermarket, and odd bits of sweet wrappers, blown by the wind, get tangled in the flowerbeds. There is a sign for a gym, which promises to give you the body you've always dreamed of, but no one seems to be taking any notice. The concerns of the inhabitants here are not with the body beautiful. Rising up on one side of the square is a nine-storey block of flats straight out of the armpit of glorious ugly prefab sixties buildings. Inside the gloomy hallway an elderly gentleman mutters about being stuck in the lift the other day

1 Message left by Diana on Simone Simmons' answerphone

---

and preferring to take the stairs, and the place has a feeling of boarded-up desolation.

There would not be much to distinguish it from most other urban developments of this era were it not for the fact that one of its inhabitants formed a unique friendship with the most famous woman in the world; a friendship that was kept quiet between the two of them until after Diana's death.

In contrast to the greyness of the hall and staircase, the flat of the woman who lives here is alive with an exotic jungle of colours that assault the senses. Bright yellow walls mix with orange sofas, and lilac furniture. The curtains are red. Lining the shelves in the entrance hall and sitting room is a dizzying array of crystals of all shapes and sizes. Where others may have porcelain figures and glassware, the ornaments in this woman's life are there for a purpose – she believes fervently in their healing powers.

The whole apartment is no bigger than a ship's cabin, and in the middle of the lounge floor sits the woman herself: cross-legged and surrounded by her three cats, Precious, Ploopsey and Sooty.

She has wild bohemian red hair and eyes that hold you with their grey-green stare. Her name is Simone Simmons, and Diana referred to her as her 'secret weapon'.

She has a disarming honesty about her; there's no edge or aloofness or suspicion here. She also speaks in straightforward, down-to-earth language, and in Diana's mind no one would have suspected the two of them could have been as close as they were.

Isolated from the Royal Family, and following her formal separation from Charles at the end of 1992, Diana had begun to turn her back on the Establishment, and the attempt to try to define her sense of self and her identity had gained an added sense of urgency.

Diana started to build an alternative court around her, which included many astrologers and therapists. Increasingly she began to lean on the members of her new court, as an escape from her loneliness, forming close friendships that were far removed from Royal circles. Simone and Diana first met through a mutual friend at a London healing centre. It was around the time of Diana's dramatic announcement on 3 December 1993 that she was withdrawing from public life, stating the reason as being the overwhelming media attention, especially to her personal life, which was 'hard to bear'. In that spirit she asked to be given the 'time and space that has been lacking in recent years'.

It is not hard to see how Diana must have found Simone Simmons a soothing antidote to her own life. Before long, humour and good-natured gossip spill naturally into any conversation with Simone.

Forty-four-year-old Simmons was born in Hampstead. She worked as a medical secretary before becoming a full-time energy healer in 1990.

Her small flat in the working-class north London suburb of Hendon is a world away from the glamour and glitz of Kensington Palace. The very first time that Diana invited her over to the Kensington Palace, Simmons wasn't even sure where it was and had to ask for the address.

'Just call me Diana,' said the Princess at that first meeting, to which the healer replied, 'Well, you can just call me Simone!'

Simmons then apologized, saying she would have to take her shoes off as her feet were killing her. She had dressed up in her smartest clothes for the occasion, but that would be the first and last time. 'In future,' she said, 'you'll have to get used to my normal self!'

The friendship between Diana and Simone Simmons started off on a purely professional basis. On the afternoon they met, before Simone's first visit to the Palace, she remembers Diana being very agitated, and unable to keep still. Simmons felt the Princess was suffering terrible emotional pain, self-doubt and self-blame for everything that was going wrong in her life.

According to Simone, 'three great truckloads of emotional waste' were extracted during that first session alone.

The scars of self-mutilation were evident on her upper arms and thighs, and in the view of her new therapist, Diana was punishing herself constantly whilst doing everything she could to please other people.

'Diana had this very bad habit of blaming herself for anything that went wrong in her emotional life. And then she would start hurting herself, first of all to get the pain out on a physical level, and secondly to see if anybody would take any notice, and give her a little bit of attention.'

As the two women talked more, Diana invited Simmons over to her apartment at Kensington Palace to cleanse or exorcise it of residual bad energy from her marriage; and a relationship that began on a patient–healer basis soon developed into a very special friendship.

Viewed from the outside, the friendship between Diana and Simone Simmons seems to have been an unlikely meeting of minds; there appears to be nothing in common, no shared territory. However, at the heart of the friendship lay Diana's desire to lead a normal life away from the goldfish bowl of public scrutiny, doing ordinary things like everyone else. Quite simply, Diana yearned for a sense of normality, and she found she could 'be herself' with her new friend, and through Simmons's recollections a picture of Diana's wish to live an ordinary life emerges.

Evenings shared with Simone would be spent mostly in Diana's 'little lounge' at Kensington Palace. There were two settees at right angles, a rug, and in front of the fireplace was a giant stuffed cushion in the shape of a hippopotamus where Simone would lounge. Together the two women would simply watch television, or spend time talking and gossiping, often until the early hours of the morning. The two women would drink tea – not from bone china cups and saucers but from 'proper mugs, not the ones reserved for formal occasions'.

Simmons tells how Diana was a complete television soap addict. 'She loved *EastEnders*, and on a Saturday night during *Casualty* there was to be no disturbance.' If the two didn't watch the episodes together, Diana would often ring Simone after *Coronation Street* and *Brookside* to exchange notes about the programmes.

One Saturday morning Diana rang Simone and said, 'What are you doing later, do you want to come over for dinner?' Simone asked her what she had in. Diana said she didn't have anything; the staff had only left her with some salad. Simone suggested there must be some dried pasta and maybe tins of tomatoes, the kinds of things you tend to find in the cupboards of most normal kitchens. But Diana assured her there was nothing there at all.

Simone promised she would buy a few things from the supermarket and drop by at around six o'clock together with their mutual friend Ursula Gatley, who was Diana's colonic therapist.

When they arrived at the Palace the two friends were introduced to Richard Kay from the *Daily Mail*. Diana then showed the two women into her kitchen, and soon Diana's friends were busy chopping vegetables and herbs. Diana just stood back and watched in complete amazement. While the pasta was on the boil, Ursula went to the bathroom, but accidentally pressed the panic button instead of the light switch. Immediately six policemen stormed inside the kitchen and went through an elaborate, well-rehearsed routine to make sure everything was all right.

Security embarrassments over, Simone decided to take a quick peep inside some of Diana's kitchen cupboards, and to her surprise discovered that one of them was crammed full of huge, catering-size packets of pasta, and in another she discovered stacks of tins of tomatoes! Diana had simply never thought to look in the cupboards and hadn't a clue all this food was there! She was awestruck by Simone's find. 'It was as though we had struck gold.'

It was the first of many such meals cooked in the KP kitchen. Afterwards they would do the washing up, a task that Diana thoroughly enjoyed.

Simmons recalls how housework became a labour of love for the Princess; she never saw it as a chore. On one occasion after they had eaten Diana opened a drawer and looked at the silver, saying, 'That's the way the staff do it'. And then she washed everything up, polished it and said, 'This is the way *I* do it.' As if to underline the point, Diana proceeded to rifle through all the kitchen drawers, pulling out anything that her staff had cleaned, then washing and polishing them all over again until they gleamed. The healer recalls how Diana enjoyed scrubbing her own bath.

Diana also revelled in the ironing – surely one of the most hated domestic rituals for anyone else. She took real pleasure from the simple act of getting rid of the creases; it was as though she was bringing a smoothness to her own existence. Housework gave Diana that longed-for sense of purpose and brought her into contact with a bit of normality.

Diana retained a sense of childishness – Simone recalled how Diana loved banisters. As a child at Park House she had whooped with joy as she slid down the long hall banister. At Kensington Palace the banisters were sprayed with furniture polish for added smoothness and speed. The spindles that jutted out half-way down would annoy Diana, as they impeded the length of her run, but she still managed the bits in between, and encouraged her boys to join her. Often she would sit on a silver tray as if it was a sledge and toboggan down the stairs.

Like many women Diana was perpetually worried about lines and wrinkles and everything else linked with the ageing process. She and Simone would discuss bubble baths, essential oils that were calming, and make-up that might make her look younger.

The healer was seeing the real Diana – the woman underneath the veneer of the Princess. She remembers with fondness one particular time that she turned up at Kensington Palace. Diana opened the door to her apartment . . . 'I'd never seen Diana like that before. She still had the mudpack on her face. All I could see were these two eyes staring out at me, and she was saying, "Mmm mmm." She couldn't talk; she didn't want it to crack whilst it was setting. Then she ended up in hysterics and it cracked anyway.'

Simone used to go for walks with Diana on Hampstead Heath together with her butler, Paul Burrell, and Richard Kay. 'When we were out walking, people used to look at the group of us, look at Diana, think, "Oh", look at the rest of us, and think, "No, it can't be, it must be a Diana double".'

The early days of the friendship were not without their hiccups. Simone is a dab hand at getting lost, and her poor eyesight means she cannot see well in the dark. She had driven over to Kensington Palace in the afternoon and stayed chatting until quite late. When it was time to go Simone climbed into her car and drove off. Diana ran out after her shouting 'Stop! Stop!' Simone had just driven through the front garden of Kensington Palace leaving tyre tracks right across the front lawn.

One evening, Diana was all by herself in the Palace apartment, and panicking. She rang Simone and said, 'Simone, I think there's a bad spirit in the house.' Asked to elaborate, she said, 'Well, there's a very funny smell. Could it be some dangerous lurking spirit?' Simone asked where the smell was coming from, but Diana had no idea. 'Right,' said Simone, 'I'll stay on the phone while we follow its trail and find where it comes from.'

And so, armed with her cordless phone, Diana tiptoed around her apartment from room to room. 'It comes from my lounge,' she declared, and then, 'No, it isn't, it's going through to the big lounge' and 'Oh, no, it's in the dining room . . . No, that's it, it's in the kitchen.'

Simone asked, 'What is the last thing you did there?' Diana couldn't remember every detail, but she said she had tried a spot of cooking earlier on; she had made some bacon sandwiches for some friends, and some tea. Simone asked, 'What then?' Diana replied, 'Well, some silly member of the staff forgot to blow out the pilot light, so I did that.' Simone almost choked. 'You're joking; you blew out the pilot light? It's supposed to stay on all the time!' 'I didn't know that,' admitted Diana sheepishly.

Simone thought her friend should call the gas board, but Diana disagreed. 'If I did that, it would be all over the front page of the papers in no time.' Simone suggested telling the police outside, but Diana didn't like that plan either, as it meant the rest of the Kensington Palace inhabitants would find out about her gaffe. Finally Simone advised her to open all the windows, to shut the door and leave a note at the back entrance for Paul Burrell to pick up in the morning, explaining what had happened. Clearly Diana followed instructions because in the morning Simone received a phone call from Burrell saying, 'You'll never believe this. The boss blew out the pilot light but she had the presence of mind to open all the windows so we weren't gassed and there wasn't an explosion in the morning!'

Diana came to depend on Simmons more and more, and when she wasn't there with her in the Palace Diana would invariably be chatting on the phone with her, giving her a run-down of the day. For the last two years of Diana's life, Simmons became the confessor, the sounding board and sister figure all rolled into one.

At the beginning Diana escaped her feelings of despair through telephone calls to her new friend.

Simone, it's Diana, I'm on my way to Terminal Four now, got so much to tell you, but I think you might have gone ghost hopping in that house, anyway I'll have this thing switched back at one, whatever, whatever, I'll catch you later, lots of love, Simone. Bye.

Simmons recalls how when she first met Diana, she pulled so many phones out of her bag. 'She had four!' This was because she thought if she was in one area where there was no reception with one network, then she must be able to get it on another network. Also it allowed Diana to take more than one call at a time.

Her friend says she always felt the need to communicate what she was thinking and what she felt, and so the two women would talk at any hour of the night or day. The calls would begin first thing in the morning when her hairdresser arrived, and then when the letters were sorted they would chat again. They would chat further in the evenings, and often continue into the early hours of the morning. But the calls started to become obsessive in their nature. Frequently they used to talk up to ten, twelve hours at a go. Even when Diana was out of the country Simmons would get a call every single day.

Hello, sorry, that was Magdi on line, I'll speak to you in the morning, lots of love, Simone. Bye.

In retrospect, Simmons describes the phone bills as 'phenomenal', 'positively disgusting, disgraceful'.

'Diana used to get four-figure bills per month, and for me sometimes it came very close to that. I think the longest call lasted about fourteen hours and she was very up and down. She started off very distressed and then we talked through that one and then we just went on to loads of other things, then she went back to being distressed; she needed a lot of reassurance.'

Simone Simmons was by no means Diana's only close friend during the final years; but she was free of ties and available for Diana much of the time and was able to help her through emotional and domestic crises without being demanding in return.

Diana drew on other friends in different ways for different reasons, but it was rare that Diana's friends would bump into each other, and most simply never got to know the others. Many of her friends note that Diana carved out very precise 'boxes' for people, and that she was very possessive about them.

Devorik tells of how he saw Rosa Monckton more at Tiffany's in London, where she was managing director, than he saw her at the Palace, and yet Rosa was also a close and trusted friend of the Princess of Wales. But Devorik never lunched or dined with Monckton. 'There were days when Diana would lunch one day at Rosa's house, and the following day at my house, that was the way Diana operated.'

Diana put her entire being into a friendship because she felt that she needed a family substitute. Consequently all her friends became her family substitutes.

To be a friend to Diana was unlike being a friend to anyone else. Lana Marks, an American accessories designer who befriended the Princess in 1996, recalls how she was asked formally by Lucia Flecha de Lima, wife of the Brazilian ambassador to Washington, 'if I would consider being a friend of the Princess of Wales and I realized at the time that this was really quite all-embracing. It wasn't just a matter of going down to the local restaurant and having coffee, but it was being there for her.'

There were certain ground rules, often unspoken. Diana was often incredibly demanding, and could prove extremely frustrating. She needed her friends to be available for her whenever it suited her. 'It was like she was saying, "I want you to be there for me twenty-four hours a day", even though she never uttered such words,' says Simone Simmons.

Her friends became props – crutches for her own insecurity – and she turned to them constantly for reassurance. These friendships were not just a one-way street – Diana was often there to give comfort and support to friends in need and was both compassionate and practical. But she also had a darker side, which could easily sour friendships, sometimes permanently. Her real need was not to have events taken out of her control. She found it difficult to accept criticism, and she demanded loyalty above all else. 'If she had an inkling or a suspicion that somebody was being slightly disloyal, that was it, she would just switch off. Even if it was just a feeling with nothing solid to base it on,' says Simmons. Penny Thornton goes on to say, 'If somebody suggested something she didn't want to hear, she took that as a disloyal statement. In other words, to people who probably wanted to help her most, and were keen to help her, if anything sounded like criticism or she was headed in the wrong direction, she would say, "How can you be disloyal, you are not being a friend, you are not being supportive." There was an extraordinary megalomania and omnipotence there, and when it came down to it, if you didn't say what she wanted to hear, you were dropped; if you were going to do anything that could be seen to put her in a bad light, that had to stop.'

The root problem was that Diana didn't really trust anyone, even her friends; she had low self-esteem, and so she found criticism especially unsettling.

Over the years she dropped many people who had once been very close to her simply because the friend had said or done something which Diana considered to be a betrayal. A lot of the time, however, Diana discovered she had been wrong, but she hated apologizing. Instead she would just phone up and say to whoever was suddenly and unexpectedly back in favour again, 'Hi, it's Diana, am I disturbing you?', and simply carry on as though nothing untoward had ever happened.

Rosa Monckton, who remained close to Diana until the end, also refers to Diana's 'dark side' in *Requiem: Diana Princess of Wales 1961–1997*. 'As a wounded animal she could be terrifying . . . it was born of some basic desire to hurt those who she felt had betrayed her.' The two women lost touch after Rosa scolded her for her 'sulky' behaviour on a royal tour of Korea with Charles in November 1992. Four months later, Diana picked up the telephone and said, 'Rosa, how are you?' It was if nothing had happened.

Debbie Frank compares Diana's behaviour to a kind of bulimia. 'Having bulimia there is this theme in your life about intensely, obsessively gorging on something; whether that's friendship, food or whatever, and then it's all too much and you have to get rid of it. So she did discard quite a lot of people through her life, and change her telephone number frequently.'

Far from being submissive and selfless, Diana could be volatile, unruly and capable of pulling the most amazing stunts if she felt threatened or denied. Diana went as far as betraying her own friends. 'If she did it once she did it a hundred times,' said Penny Thornton. 'She was two faced; she did one thing with one hand and another thing with the other. She'd say one thing to your face to reassure you, and then do something totally different, with a view to covering herself on all sides.' Talking about this side of herself, she once said to Roberto Devorik, 'Roberto, please please let's try not to be too close to each other because the people who become too close to me get destroyed.'

In part this dumping of friendships may have been a self-defence mechanism, doing the damage to others before they had a chance to do it to her, a means of protecting herself, but her actions left a trail of damage in their wake. 'She wreaked havoc on people,' says Penny Thornton. 'If there was a single trait that people who had helped her or who felt close to her felt was a flaw it was that one. You could take hysterics, you could take constant demands on your time, constant question-ing and insecurity, you could take all of that, but the way she dropped those closest to her was terrible, really terrible because she seemed to have no discrimination there at all.'

At her worst Diana was manipulative, treacherous and decept-ive. Even if these traits were manifested in order to protect herself and survive, they still left many scarred. Penny Thornton knows from bitter experience what it was like to be on the receiving end of Diana's darker side. Penny was Diana's confidante for six years from 1986 to 1992, sometimes speaking on the phone two or three times within a few days. As her astrologer, Penny developed a closeness to Diana, who would open up about matters of the heart. It was a relationship built on trust. As such her client was someone Penny wanted to protect, but she was to find it was the client who dumped on her.

Penny started working at *Today* newspaper in January 1992. On 9 March of that year she had a lengthy conversation with Diana during which the Princess confided to her that the marriage of the Duke and Duchess of York was on the rocks. On 22 March an article in the *Sunday People* reported the conversation almost verbatim making it appear as if Penny had blown Diana's confidentiality by speaking to a 'male friend' about their conversation. Horror-struck Penny wrote to Diana immediately saying she was shocked and horrified by the article and just didn't know how the information had come out. 'Maybe the phones were bugged,' she suggested as a possible explanation.

Interestingly Diana never responded to Penny's letter, even though she normally replied to her straight away. Looking back there is no doubt in Penny's mind that it was Diana herself who leaked the information about Sarah and Andrew because she wanted the story to come out. The article about the marriage breakdown coincided with the publication of a book by Lady Colin Campbell called *Diana in Private*, which was being serialized by the *Daily Express* and which was critical of the Princess, talking about her weaknesses and behavioural problems.

Diana had wanted to deflect any criticism about her by attempting to manipulate the headlines, and Penny was being used as a scapegoat. A relationship that had remained solid for six years was suddenly over for good; Diana was prepared to sacrifice her friendship with Penny in order to protect herself, unconcerned whether the other person was publicly humiliated or not. 'She was being manipulated, but she was manipulating back,' says Penny. 'She was utterly devious, she plotted, she thought she would play everybody at their own game. She would be hurt and damaged, and she was definitely not going to lie down and take it, she was going to play the media at their own game, and although you can't blame her in some ways for that, she wasn't discriminating enough to see where she should draw the line, she was incapable of perceiving real loyalty and trust.'

Many observed that Diana wasn't fair with money, and appeared to have a 'funny attitude' towards it. The truth was she had no grasp of what money meant, and forgot that 'ordinary' people had rent and bills to pay. She had a very unrealistic sense of the value of money. She liked to give people presents in place of cash.

Penny Thornton says they never discussed finances, and she never gave the Princess a bill. After the first meeting Diana gave

Penny a present of a small silver box with a bee on top, and followed it up with flowers and after that it was understood this was the way financial matters would be settled.

Simone Simmons, however, tells how she once sent Diana a bill for three months' healing which came to six hundred pounds. Diana rang up and said, 'What's this? I think we need to talk about it.' Simone duly went round to the Palace, and explained that the healing had to be paid for as it was her livelihood, and that when they first met it was on a professional basis. Instead of paying the bill, Diana offered Simmons a compact disc player. Simmons said, 'That's not much use to me, I already have one.' Diana responded, 'Well, take another one so you can play music in different parts of the house!' Of course, Diana had never been to Simmons' flat so she had absolutely no idea how tiny it was. There was no way that a second CD player could be of any practical use. In the end the bill was torn up, as Simmons didn't want to upset the friendship. To this day there are still therapists whose bills remain unpaid.

Diana had a mercurial temper. When she considered things hadn't been done right, she would stand with fists clenched by her side, go very red in the face, and scream like a four-year-old child yelling at its mother.

When she was a child at Park House, she used everything she had learned in her drama classes to attract everyone's attention. It seemed little had changed.

And it wasn't only in her friendships that such dramatic extremes of Diana's personality were to be exhibited. She projected the same behavioural repertoire into her relationships with men.

6

'I am destroyed, I am destroyed!'

The telephone rang at wealthy art dealer Oliver Hoare's home in Chelsea in January 1994. 'Hello, who's calling? Who's there?' he asked. There was nothing but an eerie silence from the other end of the line. It was just the latest in a series of anonymous calls that had been made to his home, but police equipment was already monitoring it, and the call would be traced to Kensington Palace.

On one occasion an exasperated Hoare shouted down the phone, 'Diana, is that you?' There was a crying sound from the end of the line, and the caller rang off. After this the calls stopped but only for a few days before they resumed.

Oliver Hoare was a dealer in Islamic art, and had been head of the Islamic Art department at Christie's auction house in London. Diana had first met him almost ten years previously at a party in Windsor, where he and Prince Charles had struck up a friendship based on their mutual fascination with Eastern mystical religions.

When the Wales's marriage showed signs of collapse in 1991, Hoare reputedly tried to help Diana understand Prince Charles, but abandoned his efforts when the rift between the Waleses proved irreparable. By 1992 Diana had become besotted with Hoare, and he in turn appeared to have been fascinated with her.

It was through Oliver Hoare that Diana was to meet another figure who became an important confidante in the last years of her life.

To the east of Sloane Square in Chelsea, in the chic and wealthy enclave of Belgravia, is the apartment of Lady Elsa Bowker. Elsa was born in Cairo to a French mother and a Lebanese father. After the Second World War she married James Bowker, a British diplomat, and they lived together in Burma, France, Germany and Spain before returning to Britain. On the walls of her apartment are two huge oil portraits of herself and her former husband, and numerous photographs of official embassy functions, together with pictures snapped in carefree moments during their younger days.

The rooms are ornate, lavishly decorated, and smell sumptuous. One round table is covered with hundreds of small beautifully decorated boxes; everything is rich but tasteful.

Lady Bowker has an indomitable spirit, a voice full of passion, which contains echoes of the way she has embraced life, and from time to time her eyes light up with playful mischief belying her years.

Although in her eighties and somewhat frail, her diary is a testament to her popularity: it is always full. To Diana, Lady Bowker came to represent a mother figure.

Lady Bowker had known Diana's father, Johnnie Spencer, and met the teenage Diana Spencer for the first time at Althorp, the seat of the Spencer family in Northamptonshire. She met her again at Oliver Hoare's invitation at the end of November 1993, when he brought Diana to dinner at Lady Bowker's apartment at a time when the relationship between Diana and Hoare had provoked a crisis in his marriage.

In her three-year relationship with Hoare, Diana exhibited a pattern of acutely insecure behaviour typical of all her relationships to that point. There were the obsessive telephone calls, made as early as eight o'clock in the morning or as late as midnight to Hoare's home; sometimes as many as twenty in a week.

Hoare's chauffeur Barry Hodge reported in the *News of the World* on 26 February 1995 that Diana would sometimes call twenty times in a single day.

Her friend, Roberto Devorik, described Diana's insatiable need for love. 'Nothing was ever enough. She was like the poor man who becomes a multimillionaire who is always afraid to spend any of his new-found millions, because he remembers the time when he didn't have the money even to pay the electricity bill.'

When a relationship wasn't moving forward, instead of being able to stand back and take a broader view Diana would resort to panic telephone calls, constantly ringing anyone and everyone who would listen, and who could offer advice.

Her insecurity fed her imagination, and that in turn drove her to an obsessive pursuit of those she loved. It even went as far as stalking her men. According to Simone Simmons Diana would sit outside Oliver Hoare's house for hours on end until she saw him, even if all she would earn for her trouble was a meagre glimpse.

An extension of this obsessive fear of losing people was Diana's tendency to throw herself into the task of learning as much as possible about the area of work her man was involved in, as well as everything else she could discover about his life and passions which would, she felt, make her appear more desirable to know. In Oliver Hoare's case it was Islamic philosophy. With James Hewitt, she soaked up as much radio and television coverage of the Gulf War as possible, as well as digesting heavy volumes on military strategy.

Mother figures were extremely important to Diana, and whenever she was in a relationship she would seek to befriend the mother. She visited Hewitt's mother in Devon, and Hoare's mother in London.

In difficult periods during a relationship Diana would use go-betweens to help her smooth things over. A journalist friend would apparently take letters to James Hewitt in the Gulf, and

Lady Elsa Bowker says she became the go-between for her and Oliver Hoare.

Elsa remembers sadly how failed relationships only deepened Diana's unhappiness, her sense of loneliness and insecurity. The more rejected she felt, the greater the demands on her men became; her love was totally demanding and possessive. 'If Diana was in love, the person in love with her had to abandon family, children, situation, everything and live only for her. I told her this does not happen. No man can give up everything; it's not possible,' says Elsa.

At such times, Diana's behaviour could be self-destructive. She would pick up a fork and lacerate herself. Even as late as 1994 lacerations were visible on her arms, legs and chest. Inflicting external physical injury on herself was often Diana's way of dealing with the internal, emotional pain but in the process she would also hope that somebody – anybody – would take notice and give her a little bit of attention. She displayed extreme moods, and could be emotionally volatile.

Lady Bowker recalls one Sunday when she was preparing to go to church. The telephone rang, and it was Diana insisting she had to see her there and then. Lady Bowker said she was just about to leave for church, which would be followed by lunch, but she would see her later in the afternoon when she returned home.

Diana duly turned up and rang on the bell, and Lady Bowker went downstairs to greet her. As she descended she could hear loud sobbing noises coming from the stairwell. She rushed downstairs as fast as she was able to find Diana in a dreadful state. Lady Bowker held her in her arms and asked, 'What is it?' Diana said, 'I am destroyed, I am destroyed.'

Diana was sobbing so hard after they reached the apartment that, according to Lady Bowker, she got through five entire boxes of tissues, and her great racking sobs could be heard throughout the building. Diana had just realized that her infatuation with Hoare was never going be reciprocated in the way she had desperately hoped.

'I thought that day she was going to kill herself,' says Lady Bowker, and would only let her go home to Kensington Palace when the crying had finally subsided and she had extracted a promise that Diana wouldn't do anything silly.

However, what was even more surprising to Lady Bowker was Diana's ability, following such an emotional outburst, to put on a sunny façade literally overnight, switching floods of tears into peals of laughter.

The very morning following this incident, Lady Bowker heard through a friend that Diana had gone shopping and was 'laughing her head off' as she bought shirts and ties at Turnbull and Asser, seemingly without a care in the world. On another occasion, Diana had been at a dinner party with Lady Bowker and three other friends, and was 'on cracking form', laughing all evening, only for Lady Bowker to later hear that she had left the party and was found crying her heart out in Regent's Park.

Diana became convinced that whenever she fell in love she would end up being betrayed and hurt. She had a permanent sense of unrequited love, of never being able to have what she really wanted. She was convinced that she was never loved for herself. Whenever Diana entered a relationship she was emotionally very needy right from the outset.

One of the strategies Diana developed to cope with her emotional difficulties was to seize control over those aspects of her life she *could* control. She would try to make everything she did as perfect as possible in order that she and others could approve of her. It was a simplistic strategy that stemmed from her childhood belief that she was not loved for herself, a belief that had only been strengthened as time went on. However, her lack of self-esteem meant that she could never win enough approval to counter her constant sense of failure.

One of the ways of coping with a lack of self-esteem is by doing things that other people admire – it makes us feel we are worth something. If Diana's strategy was to work, she had to tackle the problem of low self-esteem by finding things she could do well that others would then love her for. To some extent she discovered the correct route through her charity work and other high-profile projects. And she tackled them absolutely head-on.

Roberto Devorik talks about how he went through horrendous things with her. 'Seeing people burnt and without faces in hospitals, Diana would touch them in a way that I would find impossible, even though I felt very sorry; you have to have a special stomach for such things. But she was mesmerizing. One day as we were coming out of a hospital I said, "Diana, how can you do this?" and she answered, "I don't know, Roberto, it's something that gives me so much peace, so much strength".'

Her charity work gave Diana something back. According to Debbie Frank, 'She could relate to anybody who was suffering; there was a core connection there. Somehow she felt that they would understand her pain and she definitely understood theirs. So all the barriers came down, she felt tremendous empathy with people who were wounded, people who were victimized, people who suffered because *she* had suffered so much.'

According to Penny Thornton, a schism was developing between her outer successful self and her inner insecure core.

'Diana was getting public adulation for who she was and what she wore; at the same time this gap between the feeling that she wasn't really loved for herself created this division between success and achievement and handling the real world very well on the one hand, and her own interior life in chaos and not liking herself very much, actually even hating herself. As she grew older the gap between how she felt about herself as a person, and the successful outer life grew bigger and bigger. It was never breached no matter how many capable and wonderful therapists she saw; they were never able to get her to resolve this.'

Penny Thornton believed that Diana had a kind of emotional Loch Ness, and she doubts whether any one person could have ever filled the emotional gap that Diana felt within her. 'As the years went by the gap got deeper and deeper. The ability to go out on her own and carve her own independent path and public life got more successful, yet her irrational behaviour when her relationships went sour and the chaos they often gave rise to was a clear illustration that this was not a problem that was being healed; it was a problem that was ever increasing. Her work and her personal life were at separate ends of the spectrum and there seemed to be nothing in between except this void that she was continually searching to try and fill.'

After the so-called 'phone pest' scandal broke in August 1994, Hoare opted to say nothing. When Hoare's former chauffeur Barry Hodge went to the *News of the World* alleging details of an affair between Hoare and Diana in February 1995, Hoare again made no public comment.

Oliver Hoare rang up Lady Bowker at her Belgravia apartment. 'Are you in?' he asked, 'I want to bring you a letter for Diana.'

Hoare arrived with the letter and a box of cufflinks that used to belong to Diana's father. He asked Lady Bowker to return them to the Princess. At the same time, Lady Bowker received a call from Diana telling her that she had wanted Hoare to leave his wife and children, but her hopes for a future with Hoare had been dashed. Lady Bowker told Diana about the letter and cufflinks. The Princess said she would send her butler, Paul Burrell, to collect the cufflinks but she didn't want to read the letter.

Four days later Diana telephoned again, and Lady Bowker reminded her about the letter. Diana replied, 'Will you tear it up?' 'But don't you want to read it?' 'No!' answered Diana. She said she had received the cufflinks, which Elsa Bowker had sent back with butler Paul Burrell. Lady Bowker tried again. 'You can't tear up a letter from a man you have loved like this without so much as an explanation.' But Diana was adamant.

Not long after that Hoare paid another visit, asking whether Lady Bowker had given Diana his letter, only to be told the Princess didn't want it.

Lady Bowker opened it. 'It was a beautiful letter. He thanked Diana for giving him the cufflinks, but as they were such treasures he couldn't possibly keep them.'

It was February 1995, and Diana was thirty-four years old. Friendships and relationships had come and gone, and in her relentless search for stability and love, Diana had opened up to friends from many walks of life; she had embraced all sorts of healing and therapy. Her life was a therapeutic treadmill littered with failed love interest.

With Oliver Hoare, as with many others, Diana had failed to find a future, but the chapter had brought with it an enhanced interest in the mysteries of the East, a part of the world which seemed to hold some deep fascination for Diana.

Although her interest in religion was almost zero, during the time she knew Oliver Hoare Islam and Islamic philosophy, especially Sufism, had captivated Diana. Sufism is the mystical, inner philosophy of Islam. Its message of 'peace with all' has long drawn Muslims and non Muslims alike. Diana was even photographed in April 1994 reading *Discovering Islam*, a book by a Cambridge University professor, Akbar Ahmed, on the balcony of a chalet whilst on a skiing holiday at Lech in Austria.

Her friendship with Oliver Hoare had led her to feed hungrily on the culture of the East. She could not have known then, but her relationship with the East and with Islam was destined to continue. In little more than eight months' time she would meet and be attracted to another man who was part of the very culture she was now soaking up. A man who would act as a new force in her life, providing a powerful influence that would reshape the Princess, someone who would help her to start breaking the vicious circle of insecurity that had haunted her for so long.

Part Two
Prelude to a Romance

Diana's interest in the mysticism and culture of the East, even during her time with Oliver Hoare, was not born out of a whim. Its roots lay further back in her life. Only in retrospect can we begin to understand why Pakistan became so important to her.

7

'What can I do to help?'

It was a splendid July morning in 1990, nine years after Diana had got married and a year before she was to meet the dealer of Islamic art, Oliver Hoare. Professor Akbar Ahmed, of the Faculty of Oriental Studies, was sitting in his study at Selwyn College in Cambridge, when the telephone rang.

Three years earlier Professor Ahmed had been invited by the government of Pakistan and Selwyn College to accept the Iqbal Fellowship in Cambridge, and as a result he had become involved in the debate on Islam, and in particular the future of Islam in Britain.

His involvement with the debate coincided with a letter dated 27 June 1990 that had just arrived at the London head-quarters of the Royal Anthropological Institute. The letter was from Diana's private secretary at the time, Patrick Jephson. It was addressed to the Institute's director, Jonathan Benthall, and informed him that the Princess would be pleased to accept an invitation to visit the Institute's offices in Fitzroy Street and that she would be grateful if this engagement could include a briefing on Pakistan.

Benthall, who was already acquainted with Ahmed, got straight on the phone to the Professor in Cambridge and told him of the request to give a private briefing on Pakistan for the Princess of Wales. He asked whether the Professor would be prepared to speak at such an event. The Professor accepted instantly. Although he had never met the Princess, he felt pleased and excited by the prospect of talking to someone who was so eminent and who had such a high public profile. The two men agreed that an introduction to Islam would be an appropriate topic to be covered at the briefing.

Two months later, on Thursday 13 September 1990, Professor Ahmed made his way to the Royal Anthropological Institute, in Fitzroy Street, London, wearing a traditional shalwar kameez.

Ahmed was extremely curious about Diana. 'I felt she was an intelligent person, yet the media often gave her a rough time. I felt I could make an impact with her if I could somehow "get through".'

The lecture on Islam was due to be held in the general office on the ground floor of the Institute. Promptly, at three thirty, Diana arrived and was directed to a seat on the front row, just below the lectern.

Professor Ahmed describes it as an enormously memorable occasion, not least because it was most unusual for a member of the Royal Family to be lectured to in this way – with Diana seated on a chair whilst the speaker stood *above* her at the lectern.

At the time of the lecture, tensions in the Gulf were at their highest. Only five weeks earlier, on 2 August, Saddam Hussein had invaded Kuwait, and there was a lot of anti-Islamic sentiment in the British newspapers. Not knowing the Princess, Ahmed wasn't sure of the kind of reception he would receive. He needn't have worried. Although Diana was dressed in her most business-like fashion, in a pin-stripe suit, Ahmed remembers her ability to put everyone at ease. Her body language, and the expression in her eyes, was very attentive, and his own anxiety immediately disappeared.

'The combination of her tremendous physical presence, her vulnerability and her shyness I found to be quite overwhelming,' he says.

Ahmed decided to pitch the lecture at a more human level. 'I began by saying if the Royal Person expected me to whip out a copy of the *Satanic Verses* from the recesses of my Oriental robes and burn it, then she would be quite disappointed!

'There was a flicker of a smile on Diana's face, and this set the tone for the rest of the talk.' Professor Ahmed challenged the stereotype images of Islam as a religion of book-burners, hostage-takers and terrorists. Instead of pursuing any political argument, Professor Ahmed chose to tell the Princess one or two stories about the holy Prophet; stories that he hoped would appeal to her on an emotional level, and display Islam in a different light.

'I told her the story of how the holy Prophet was known for his legendary kindness and gentleness, especially towards women and children. However, in the early days of Islam there was great hostility towards him in Mecca. One old woman in particular would wait for him in her room and every time he passed beneath her window as he walked along the street she would pour dirt and garbage down on him.

'One day when he passed there was no response from the old lady. On inquiring about her, the Prophet was told she was seriously ill. He immediately went up to see her and ask about her health, and how he could be of help. The old lady broke down in tears, as no one had been to see her during her illness except the man she had been trying to humiliate.

'She henceforth became a Muslim.'

Ahmed went on to challenge many of the stereotypes associated with the relationship between men and women in Islam.

'I talked about the great respect men have for women in Islam. In the Western media Islam is depicted as a religion of women-haters, wife-beaters and harems, and so on, but the reality is that Muslim men are very, very considerate to their women. Women are given a very high status, and this remains throughout history, starting from the time of the Prophet.

Women have a respected place, they have a status, and there's continuity and care. I talked to Diana about the fact that in Islam marriage is taken very seriously; it is seen as the foundation of society, a secure base for children, and a means of ensuring that core family values are carried forward to future generations. Whilst there is divorce in Islam, there is also a great emphasis on stability and coherence and respect for each other and staying together.'

Professor Ahmed highlighted several aspects of the religion that would have sent powerful messages to Diana. First of all he had spoken of the compassion of Islam, perhaps a touchy subject given the public feeling at the time. 'This seemed to generate enormous curiosity in the Royal guest,' notes Ahmed. Secondly, Islam has at its core a family structure and, says Professor Ahmed, a concern for women, and a respect for the mother figure. Bearing in mind Diana's own childhood, and the breakdown of her own marriage at this time, what Ahmed was saying undoubtedly had a resonance in her own life.

Ahmed's own impression was that Diana was not only absorbed with what was going on, and what he was saying, but was seriously prepared to respond to it.

After the lecture it had been made clear to all present that Diana would have to leave straight away for another function. In fact she found time to have a few minutes' chat with Professor Ahmed.

'She moved over to me, indicating to everyone else that this was a private conversation, and she said to me, "What can I do to help? How can I improve the understanding between Islam and the West, and what role can I play?"'

Ahmed was extremely moved by her words and replied, 'I think you can play a great role, there's a great deal of misunderstanding and that has to be removed, and only someone like you can do it.'

Ahmed admits to being astonished by Diana's response. 'Looking at it from the outside, she was the classic British Princess growing up in a certain milieu, totally cut off from the world of Islam. The Royal Family are not generally known to be mystics or scholars interested in Sufism so while there was formal *contact* with them on the subject of Islam, there was no rapport.

'With Diana, on the other hand, I felt there *was* a rapport. I think this tremendous respect, love and compassion that is supposed to be shown to women in Islam may have struck some kind of chord in her.'

The Professor could not know just how perfect and fortuitous a chord he had struck; however he had read enough about her, and was sufficiently perceptive to know that behind the interest lay something personal.

'Looking back, 1990 was the time when tensions in her own marriage were beginning to surface. There may have been a personal resonance when she was thinking that here's this civilization where there's a position for women and women are loved and given the kind of attention and care that they deserve.' Ahmed goes on to say, 'I had a feeling that she had responded; that inside her there was a tiny spark, a spark of interest in Islam itself. I think it was forcing Diana to reassess her own life, and it was forcing her to come to the conclusion that perhaps many other values, perhaps many other things that she believed in or respected in the early 1990s, were after all not so important to her.'

It is possible that her interest in the lecture may also have been connected with James Hewitt's imminent posting to the Gulf. Ever since the Iraqi invasion of Kuwait some five weeks earlier, Diana feared that Hewitt's unit, the Life Guards, might be sent into battle. She had been calling him regularly throughout the autumn whilst he awaited events in Germany, and by January 1991, as the United States, Britain and other allies prepared for war with Iraq, Diana would be tuning into news bulletins on the radio and television whenever she had a chance.

Even if that were so, she took away from the lecture far more than she had bargained for; it had hit all the appropriate buttons concerning love, women and the family. It was not the last time she was to see Professor Ahmed. Following the lecture, the Professor kept in touch with Patrick Jephson, Diana's private secretary. They talked on the phone from time to time, and shared lunch together in Cambridge.

When it was announced that Diana was going to Pakistan on a solo state visit, Jephson informed Professor Ahmed that Diana would like him to brief her.

A year after the lecture at the Royal Anthropological Institute in Fitzroy Street, in the middle of September 1991, Akbar Ahmed was to meet the Princess again; this time she was to be the hostess, inviting him to tea at Kensington Palace. The Professor nearly ended up at the wrong place, when a minicab driver who was confident he knew where to find Kensington Palace took him to Buckingham Palace instead. Fearing he would miss his appointment he jumped into a black cab and just made it with a couple of minutes to spare.

Professor Ahmed remembers Diana's warmth and informality; they met as if they were old friends. 'She was very informally dressed, just wearing jeans and a shirt,' he said.

Diana said she wanted Ahmed's advice as she prepared to go to Pakistan. The trip had actually been planned for the previous year after Diana had accepted an invitation from Benazir Bhutto, but it had to be postponed when Bhutto was deposed as Prime Minister and her twenty-month-old Pakistan People's Party government dissolved on 6 August 1990 by the country's President, Ghulam Ishaq Khan.

She was embarking on her visit to Pakistan without Charles, so it was a test of her diplomatic ability. Diana was extremely anxious about the formalities, particularly as it was a largely male-dominated society. She wanted to know what she should wear, how long her dresses should be, how she should speak, what she should say.

The last question was an easy one for the holder of the Iqbal Fellowship. Sir Allama Mohammad Iqbal is the Pakistani national poet, so Ahmed advised Diana that if she had the right opportunity she should quote Iqbal's poetry. Ahmed gave her one particular quote to remember: 'There are so many people who wander about in jungles searching for something, but I will become the servant of that person who has got love for humanity.'

8

'Do you know Imran Khan?'

The rustic, gnarled doorways spill over with colourful foodstuffs, and the air reverberates to the sound of copper, brass and silver being hammered into shape. The area throngs with humanity, and the hustle and bustle of an ancient civilization still reliant on donkeys and the horse and cart. This is the old walled city of Lahore – a warren of twisting, narrow alleyways surrounded by a nine-metre-high wall adjacent to the old fort, and the Badshahi mosque. It still looks very much like it must have done in the days of the Mogul Emperors, and the atmosphere is redolent with the history, romance and tragedy that has always attached itself to Old Lahore.

Outside the old city, Lahore is a teeming modern urban sprawl inhabited by millions, and utterly choked with traffic. It is a city with acute disparity between the wealthy minority who live in neo-classical villas, travel in chauffeur-driven cars and send their children to private schools, and the desperately poor majority whose cramped quarters criss-cross the city, and who are unwilling to send their children to school even if education *were* freely available as the money the children can earn is needed to sustain the family.

On 22 September 1991, a few days after her briefing with Professor Ahmed over tea at Kensington Palace, Diana flew to Pakistan for her five-day state visit. The country bubbled with excitement before her arrival, her face was everywhere: on walls, the windows of taxis and motor rickshaws, and hairdressers offered 'Princess Di' cuts, considered the height of fashion by Pakistan's young women. She emerged from the plane wearing a green silk dress, and that evening she was hosted by the President of Pakistan at a banquet in the presidency. Diana was seated next to the President, Ghulam Ishaq Khan. After the welcoming speech Diana, drawing on the advice given to her by Professor Ahmed, read out her own speech and included the quotation from Iqbal. It clearly impressed her hosts and was headline news all over the newspapers the following day.

Her tour began with a visit to the old city of Lahore where amongst other places on the itinerary she was to enter the Badshahi mosque. No one can fail to be awestruck by this great place of worship. It is one of the largest mosques in the world, with four tapering red minarets and three enormous marble domes. Its courtyard is capable of holding at least sixty thousand people.

When the sun is setting the mosque is at its most spectacular, the red light catching the domes, setting them ablaze like a hot furnace, throwing everything else into its shadow.

Before going to the mosque Diana was concerned about the dress code. She was wearing a scarf, but her dress was knee high. She asked her official consort if the Western clothes she was wearing would be all right for the visit to such a holy place, and she was told they would be fine.

Upon arrival at the Badshahi mosque, Diana was met by the Imam, and after they walked through the courtyard together he showed her through the sacred precincts.

Like Professor Ahmed, the Imam was very interested in Diana as a figure who could potentially unite Muslims and Christians. He informed her that during the *saleeby* wars (the Crusades) both Muslim and Christian leaders had created bloodthirsty hatred among the believers. He told her it was imperative to bridge the hatred in this century and bring about unity.

The Imam gave the Princess twelve books, including a copy of the Koran with note-slips for reference, and one book about the prophet Mohammed. She left promising that she would read the books; that she would study Islam and do her best to bring both Muslims and Christians together.

Afterwards she remarked to her consort that the Imam didn't seem to mind her short dress, and that he was very gracious and very kind to her. The consort replied, 'Of course he didn't mind, your highness, and good for him. He saw you in a short dress because the more the conservative religious people see other people from many different regions of the world wearing different garments and with different ways of behaving, the more we close the gaps and bridge the distance between us.'

By all accounts, Diana liked her consort's reply and felt reassured. However on the following day a number of hard-line mullahs protested, saying her skirt was too short, and the Imam was criticized for presenting a non-Muslim with a copy of the Koran. The case actually went to court, but it ended with the mullahs being ordered to stop wasting the judge's time.

Diana was accompanied on her five-day tour by her consort, Seyeda Abida Hussain, then a member of the newly elected Prime Minister Nawaz Sharif's cabinet and a confident, charismatic, successful middle-aged woman who had fought throughout her career to alleviate the oppression of women in this male-dominated Islamic society. They travelled to Islamabad, Peshawar and Chitral, visiting healthcare and educational institutions.

Hussain says the Princess was taken to a family planning centre, where, 'She was very sweet with the baby that she took in her lap. I warned her that the baby didn't have a nappy, and we might have a little accident and it would ruin her dress, and she looked at me and said, "Oh, I don't mind." She was very sweet.'

She was also taken to a centre for disabled children, which is run by the Pakistani army in Rawalpindi and as she talked to the children one of the military officers – a brigadier – stepped forward suddenly and said, 'My son is a doctor in the north of

England and this is his phone number and his name and address. If ever you need his services, just give him a call.'

The official party was irritated with the brigadier because he had violated the invisible cordon and by so doing breached etiquette. Diana wasn't at all fazed though; she turned to the brigadier, looked him in the eye and said, 'Oh, thank you, I will call him sometime.'

During the visit she was also taken to centres for the rehabilitation of heroin addicts, and in Peshawar she saw Sandy Gall's Centre for the Disabled, which treats victims of landmines.

Hussain describes her presence as fairytale-like. It was all pervading and meant that people all over the country – men and women – poured out onto the streets spontaneously to see her.

Diana was later to refer back to the street scenes in a letter to Hussain dated 27 September 1991, in which she confessed to feeling humbled by the large numbers of people who had flocked to see her.

Hussain says that Diana was very restrained during the first two days of the visit and did not ask any questions; she just seemed to be watching and observing everything, but by the third day she had relaxed a little and began to open up. The two women began to get to know each other.

Diana said, 'It must be so stressful and tiring for you to have to do all this with me.' 'No, actually, I'm enjoying it, but I must tell you honestly that I really didn't want the assignment because I thought it would not be at all enjoyable.' Diana looked at Hussain and asked, 'Why?', to which Hussain replied that it was mostly to do with vanity, really. 'I'm short and ample, and walking next to you who are so tall and slender I will look like a pincushion.'

Diana looked Hussain up and down and said, 'You don't look at all like a cushion, but you are as comforting as one.'

Hussain recalls Diana's sense of humour when they were travelling on an internal flight together. 'At some point we were on the plane, and she picked up the newspapers that were set on the table beside her, and she handed me *The Times* and said, "This is for you because you're intelligent", and she picked up the *Daily Mail*, and said, "This is for me, because I'm not." And I laughed and said, "Your Highness, you do yourself an injustice. I have not noticed any lack of intelligence." So she smiled very sweetly and just proceeded to look at the newspaper.'

Diana told Hussain about her boys. She said that Harry was 'very much like his father', while William was 'much more like her', and that her in-laws were 'very strict'.

'I asked her whether she cared for horses, and she said, "No, but you know, all my in-laws are very involved with horses", so we talked a little bit about that.'

Hussain recalls how Diana seemed to be in a process of self-discovery. 'It was quite clear to me that she was troubled and confused. She loved the stardom, she loved the cameras and she loved all the attention. At the same time she was unsure of herself. She seemed to be in search of a person older than herself, someone like a mother figure, that she could open up to.'

According to Hussain, Diana seemed fascinated by the Pakistani male image, the strong Muslim man. It seemed to be all she wanted to talk about. Diana was focusing not on the history or the texture of the land and the images that she was seeing, but on its people, and particularly on its men, being much less curious about the women. 'She seemed to be in great awe of men and, you know, as a middle-aged woman having conquered that feeling myself I wanted to reach out to her on that one! Being a woman and having militated against the notions of patriarchal order that prevail in large part in my country, I spotted her bias in favour of it and assured her that Muslim men are as ordinary as any other men anywhere – no worse, no better. But she seemed to find Muslim men compelling. She thought Pakistani men were very good looking, which they very often are. She admired the bearers, the waiters who serve the people in our government residences, because they are all chosen for their height, and they wear jackets with brass buttons and these elegant turbans, and she noticed them and said, "My goodness, they're so handsome!" And she noticed people in the street, she noticed the difference in the Pathans, the way this clan of people is tall and often striking in looks.'

Hussain goes on to say, 'I think she had a considerably romantic image of Muslim men. I think she was beginning to define them as great macho men, and she was attracted to the notion of the strong Muslim patriarchal type. She was interested in the notion of Muslim men being protective towards women. She appeared to be a young woman who had grown up on Mills and Boons. I am a mother of two daughters who are in their mid-twenties, who also grew up on Mills and Boons, but who left them behind by the time they had grown out of their teens. But Diana seemed to be still in the Mills and Boon state of mind and development'.

In particular Diana expressed to her new friend a desire to meet and get to know Imran Khan. Hussain recalls how she was very curious about him. 'I think she was confused as to why I myself wasn't. I connected him only to cricket and I wasn't very interested in cricket. She asked me if I knew him, and I said "Briefly", and she asked me what I thought of him, and I said, "Well, he's a cricketer!" She said that her sister Lady Sarah had known him, but she had never met him. She said she was hoping that when she came to Pakistan she would meet Imran Khan, and I said, "Well, unfortunately he's not in Pakistan, otherwise we would have arranged for him to meet with you, but he is playing cricket in Australia or somewhere." Diana said, "Imran seems to be caught between two worlds, the West and the East, and he seems to me to have a sort of spir-itual quality." I found that a little troubling in the sense that I understood from that that she had the notion that Muslim men are protective, and yes at one level they are, but at the same time they tend to be dominant and tend to subsume the persona of their spouse. Imran Khan had by that time made his social presence felt in London and he was the easiest person she could relate this notion of male protectiveness to.'

Hussain observed that Khan appeared to epitomize everything that Diana was looking for at the time. 'She was focusing on people, and he seemed to be the person she focused on. He was known in social circles, Lady Sarah knew him well, and met him at parties. She obviously thought he looked right, and at that point it seemed to me that he was the sort of mythical figure she had constructed.

'Diana was obviously looking for love, and if she did not find it in marriage, and if she had some sort of sense of disappointment with some other involvement then obviously she was looking for a man who would be safe, secure, who would perhaps have a moral code flowing from a tradition, or customs that would prevent him from disappointing her,' says Hussain.

With the collapse of her marriage to a man at the heart of the British Establishment, someone from a different world, religion and culture would be appealing and compelling to her in this sense. A Muslim who was also Westernized like Imran Khan, whether it be a Muslim who was living in Britain, or a Muslim interacting with Western culture to the extent that he was really 'global', could be doubly attractive to the Princess. Diana could be at ease with such a man, while at the same time feeling she would be escaping into a different world, into a different civilization.

It was some time before such a man would appear in Diana's life, but seeds were being sown, and Diana was clearly intrigued by the idea of a man who combined elements of the East and West .

9

'Maybe it's time!'

Calcutta is an urban horror story. The mere name conjures up visions of squalor, starvation, disease and death. They are all true, and to many people this place sums up the worst of India. The city sprawls north–south along the banks of the Hooghly River, and so do its slums. A massive influx of refugees fleeing from East Bengal, combined with India's own post-war population explosion means there is intolerable overcrowding, there are too many mouths to feed. It is not uncommon to see a child run naked through the lines of stalled cars and traffic jams looking for food, beggars in rags sleeping where they have sat all day, too hungry and weary to move. Little wonder Mother Teresa set up her Calcutta mission here in 1950 to focus on the city's festering problems.

Although there is a constant mass movement of people day and night in all parts of the city, it is not uncommon to sit for an hour in traffic that is going nowhere. The streets are clogged and the inside of a car is likely to be filled with hot sickly fumes inherited from the belching exhausts of neighbouring vehicles. The city is desperately polluted.

In a narrow cobbled alleyway off a busy main road just outside the centre of the city and south of the river, there is a thick wooden door. In the doorway there is a sign which reads 'Mother Teresa – In'. It is still there to this day.

The door opens into the courtyard of the Mother House, and

at once there is a sense of peace verging almost on tranquillity in this city of squalor and confusion. On the right-hand side, through another doorway, is the vast tomb where the Mother now lies. It was her wish to be buried here at the heart of her mission.

The eighty-five nuns of the Missionaries of Charity are dressed in white habits trimmed with blue, and are busy with their morning chores. They do their washing using metal pails, before hanging everything up to dry in the baking heat. The nuns dedicate their lives to serving the poor, irrespective of creed or colour, and there are some two hundred novices who also volunteer their services before becoming full members of the Charity. Mother Teresa's picture looks down on the assembly at various vantage points along the whitewashed walls.

On 10 February 1992, four months after her trip to Pakistan, Charles and Diana arrived in India for a six-day official visit. It was Diana's first trip to the country. They were staying in separate suites at the Presidential Palace in New Delhi. Following a visit on 11 February to Sonia Gandhi, the Italian-born widow of Rajiv Gandhi, the former premier who had been assassinated by a bomb blast the previous summer during the country's election campaigns, Charles and Diana went their separate ways. Charles visited the School of Planning and Architecture in the capital, and Diana went on a day trip to Agra. It was here that one of the most memorable images of Diana sitting alone in front of the magnificent Taj Mahal was taken.

Described as the most extravagant monument to love ever built, the Taj Mahal was constructed by Emperor Shah Jahan in memory of his second wife, Mumtaz Mahal. Her untimely death in childbirth in 1631 left the emperor so heartbroken his hair is said to have turned grey overnight.

Construction of the Taj was an epic task which took more than twenty years and the story goes that there might well have been two of them – a second one in black that would be his own tomb. But before he could embark on his second masterpiece he was deposed by his son, who was afraid that such excess would be financially crippling.

Shah Jahan spent the rest of his life imprisoned in Agra Fort, looking out along the river to the final resting place of his wife, whose body was now entombed within the monumental evidence of his own obsession about a lost love. Diana had picked her spot well.

Many years before, Prince Charles had been captivated by the romance of the Taj Mahal. This was before his marriage, and he said at the time that he would one day like to bring his future wife there. He never did, but the pledge made Diana's solo visit all the more poignant, and the press pack was determined to capture the meaningful moment on film. Diana was clearly willing to oblige. By posing alone in front of such a monument to love she was sending out a signal to the world; she was lonely and isolated and felt very much unloved, and her 'marriage was on the rocks'. It was a vivid example of her growing maturity in the art of using the media for her own ends.

The next stop, Jaipur, on 12 February, where Prince Charles was scheduled to participate in a polo match, gave rise to another potent image. After the match, Charles tried to kiss her – as the cameras looked on. But Diana was too quick for him. With a sudden twist of her head, the Prince was left planting his kiss on her neck, and cameras captured the awkward moment for posterity.

After visiting Jaipur and Hyderabad, the couple arrived in Calcutta. As Charles was due to make a private visit to Nepal, Diana remained by herself in the city, so that she could visit Mother Teresa's Missionaries of Charity. She had been hoping to meet Mother Teresa, but the eighty-two-year-old Catholic nun was absent after being admitted to a hospital in the Vatican in Rome with pneumonia and heart problems. What Diana saw in Calcutta was to have a profound effect on her.

The Hospice for the Dying, at Kalighat in the south of the city, presents a scene of pitiful suffering. Row upon row of blue mattresses line the floors of a dimly lit room with absolutely no space between them. The men and women are kept in separate rooms, but space is so short that some patients lie in corridors adjacent to the kitchens, or on ledges, wherever there is a place. The floors are stone flags, and although the nuns work tirelessly to bring some dignity to the dying, it is a desperate job.

Most of the terminally ill men and women Diana saw during her visit to the hospice were suffering from extreme malnutrition or tuberculosis.

While there she was given a tray of sweets to hand out to the patients, and as she did so, some of them clasped her hand. Diana kept saying how sad she thought it all was.

After leaving the hospice she went on to visit three hundred and fifty abandoned or orphaned infants at the Shishu Bhavan home for children; all of them had been rescued from the streets by Mother Teresa's nuns.

Diana stroked their faces and picked up one deaf and dumb thirteen-month-old boy. His name was Myso, and the Princess carried him around the nursery, cradled in her arms.

The nuns who were accompanying her revealed that the Princess said she would like to dedicate the rest of her life to helping the poor and suffering.

Someone who was watching Diana from afar was a woman who had experienced life in Calcutta nearly forty years earlier, and who understood precisely what Diana was feeling.

Tucked away in a square in Earls Court in west London, amongst a collection of hotels offering cheap bed and breakfast, is the home of a woman who was Diana's acupuncturist for six years from 1989 to 1995.

Inside the flat there is an aroma of exotic scented candles;

Eastern rugs line the floors, and various religious figures are draped with Catholic rosary beads.

In one corner of the living room there is a piano and large sash windows look out on the square.

The whole place has a homy feel. The woman who greets you is of diminutive stature, with greying hair. Her accent leaves you in no doubt that she is Irish, and her steel-grey eyes scrutinize you carefully before the door is finally opened. Her name is Oonagh Toffolo. Now in her seventies, she's a former nurse from County Sligo who at one time befriended the late Duke of Windsor during his last years in Paris, and latterly came to be a close friend of Diana's too.

Oonagh's air of formality is quickly dispelled by the twinkle in her Irish eyes and Assam tea is served from tiny Chinese cups.

'It was 5 September 1989. Diana had rung me the day before and asked if she could see me. I went, I always remember, in a green taxi. Diana was ready for my visit and greeted me with outstretched arms, in her bare feet; she was very much a nature's child. We immediately felt at home with each other. It was our quest for helping humanity really that gelled the relationship.'

Diana had first heard of Oonagh Toffolo's work through a mutual friend, Mara Berni, the owner of the San Lorenzo restaurant in Knightsbridge.

Over the years Oonagh estimates she saw Diana three hundred times, either at Kensington Palace or at her home in Earls Court. She treated Diana with needles at the back of her neck.

Oonagh remembers Diana always being so natural. On one occasion when leaving the Earls Court flat the Princess shook hands with the cleaner.

While Oonagh thought of Diana as a 'nature's child', Diana referred to Oonagh in turn as an 'earth mother'. This need for a relationship with an older woman was a recurrent theme in Diana's life because she felt abandoned by her own mother at an early age.

During the acupuncture sessions, Toffolo would talk to Diana like a teacher; she gave her a dozen books on health, healing, missionaries and martyrs and urged her to examine other religions. They became trusted friends. In between the acupuncture they talked at length about Diana's marriage to Charles. Oonagh was to witness at first hand Diana's nagging self-doubt and insecurities, which eventually gave way to the slow realization that she had an almost unique quality of compassion that could help inspire others.

As a devout Catholic woman in her late twenties Toffolo had journeyed to Mother Teresa's in Calcutta where she worked alongside the Mother helping Calcutta's sick and poor.

She recounted her travels to Diana. 'I talked about my time in India, and particularly Calcutta, and the great place India was and how much it needed to have its children looked after. And she was very impressed with this, because she had a great love of children, and to see the little children needing love was a kind of image of herself. I remember giving her *A Little Book of Hugs,* and she devoured that because it responded to her wanting to embrace the world.'

When Diana told Oonagh Toffolo about her own trip to Calcutta, Oonagh had asked her to keep a record of her thoughts and emotions while she was there.

As Diana sat in the courtyard of the Mother House, the nuns were congregated in a semicircle, whilst others looked down from crowded balconies and windows. The nuns in the courtyard launched into a chorus of 'Make all your life something beautiful for God'. As the sisters launched into their second hymn, Diana was showered with rose petals, and wiped a tear away from her eyes.

As Oonagh had requested she was indeed keeping a record of her thoughts. In the account that she wrote and later gave a copy of to her friend there are clear signs of Diana's spiritual development and her realization that she could help people.

It reveals that she wanted to be part of this great effort to bring help to humanity, and she wanted to do it on a global scale.

But it is the intensity of Diana's feelings that is the most striking feature of her written record. She confessed that it was impossible to find the right words to describe her true feelings; in fact, she said that people close to her would be frightened if she *could* describe them. She told how she now felt set apart from other people by this deep sense that she had a mission to be fulfilled. With this came responsibility and with that the power to change her life. She wondered whether it was time to do just that – change her life.

10

'Isn't he drop dead gorgeous!'

Although Diana could shed her own troubles by losing herself in others' traumas, and despite visibly strengthening whilst comforting others more fragile than she, there is no denying the genuine compassion she felt for the sick and the dying.

Roberto Devorik recalls a visit he and the Princess made to a hospital where a man was dying from AIDS. 'He was consumed by the illness, and it was very hard to look at him, his eyes were almost gone. Diana went to his bed and took his hand, and this is not just fantasy, but the eyes of the man became alive again. She didn't speak to him, she just sat holding his hand for three minutes, and then she opened her mouth and said, "You know, I think that up there we are going to have much more fun." And she kissed his hand and left the room. The man died three days later, but his mother wrote her a letter saying Diana had made him so happy, he died peacefully.'

Having discovered within herself a power of compassion for the sick and dying, over the years Diana began to believe she had a special gift. Moreover, she was now finding she was loved for something that came quite naturally; she didn't have to force it or confront anybody with it. This and her charity work weren't things that could ever lead to a betrayal.

Nineteen ninety-five saw the convergence of a number of key

events. Diana had separated from Charles, and had begun to explore life beyond the Establishment. Her relationship with Oliver Hoare was over, but she had immersed herself further into Islam and Islamic philosophy. And having discovered her ability to help others, she was reinforcing her own inner strength through charity work.

Now in September 1995 she was to make a visit to the London Royal Brompton Heart and Lung hospital that would make her life take a new course. The catalyst once again was her acupuncturist friend, Oonagh Toffolo.

In Toffolo's apartment in Earls Court, evidence of her husband who passed away in 1999 is inescapable. The music he loved, the books he read, a huge portfolio of portrait photographs bound in leather, and smaller photos are dotted around the various desks and surfaces.

As Oonagh Toffolo sits in her maroon, velvet-backed chair, surrounded by pungent lilies of the valley, her head slips over to one side and she has to support it with her hand.

She is about to embark on the story of how Diana's secret love for a Pakistani doctor came to be, and to describe the journey that started in London and took her to Lahore. But to tell that story means recalling painful memories surrounding her husband Joseph's illness. It requires her to take a deep breath to summon up the strength, and the words emerge slowly.

'Joseph had been troubled by heart problems for two or three years; so much so that in the spring of 1995 it became clear that surgery was going to be necessary.' The operation, a triple heart bypass and a valvular repair, was scheduled for 31 August, at the Royal Brompton Hospital. Diana had written Joseph a note on 5 April, letting both of them know they were in her thoughts and prayers, and that she was summoning positive energy.

Two weeks before Joseph Toffolo's surgery, on 14 August, Diana invited them for lunch, to celebrate Oonagh's birthday. After lunch Joseph, who was an accomplished singer, asked whether he could perform a song for the Princess. He chose a piece called 'La Paloma' (the dove). Diana was overwhelmed. She told him that nobody had ever sung for her like that before. He sang with such soul that she swore she could hear his heart beating. In a touching moment, she placed her own hands over Joseph's heart.

The Royal Brompton Heart and Lung Hospital is a low-rise, unprepossessing building in the heart of Chelsea. The white terraced houses lining Sydney Street opposite the hospital reflect the prosperity of their inhabitants, and the surrounding shops set the scene of privilege and affluence.

The day of the operation arrived and Joseph Toffolo said, 'I'm going to sail through this', as he disappeared into the Brompton operating theatre.

Joseph's operation was performed by the renowned surgeon Professor Sir Magdi Yacoub, who was assisted in the operating theatre by a senior registrar by the name of Mr Hasnat Khan. The procedure completed, Joseph was returned to the intensive care ward to recuperate. However he had only been there for twenty minutes when the senior ward sister noticed that his drainage jars were full of blood. Joseph was suffering a massive haemorrhage. Moments later the cardiac arrest alarm sounded. Professor Yacoub charged into the ward with his scalpel in hand and there and then re-opened his patient's chest wall. The bleeding was successfully stopped and Joseph's heart re-started. It had been touch and go.

At home, Oonagh was waiting for a call. None came, owing to a mix-up, so she rushed to the hospital. She and an old friend, Sister Mairead, were eventually allowed to see Joseph in intensive care and were shocked by how ill he looked. Oonagh telephoned Diana around nine o'clock in the evening to tell her of Joseph's critical condition.

Although by 1995 Diana had abandoned herself to faith healers, acupuncturists and alternative therapists, using them as crutches in her search for something secure to hold her life to, it wasn't just a one-way street. Now it was to be payback time, as Diana was to spring to the aid of her friend.

Oonagh continues, 'I told her of Joseph's grave condition and Diana said, "I'll be there in the morning, at ten o'clock." True to her word she arrived; I was waiting for her and took her into intensive care to see Joseph. After that we went into another little room in the unit. We were hardly there a minute when Hasnat Khan arrived with his retinue of assistants. I introduced him to Diana. He merely acknowledged her with a formal nod then proceeded to focus on Joseph's condition. It is doubtful whether the Princess of Wales had ever made less of an impression on anyone in her entire life!

'Khan came straight to the point and said Joseph's condition was very serious and he wanted my permission to take Joseph back to theatre. I looked at this kind man who I had seen many times during the night, and I said, "Do please look after Joseph because he's very precious to us", and I kissed his hand. He said he would come up later on, perhaps at two o'clock and give me a full account of what he had found. With another brief nod to the Princess he said goodbye and left the room.

'I hadn't noticed anything about Hasnat Khan except that he was a very kind man with lovely eyes and beautiful hands and that he was a caring surgeon, but after he had left the room, Diana said to me, "Oonagh, isn't he drop-dead gorgeous!"

'That was how it started. I think he made a huge impact on her. I suppose she fell in love with him, at first sight!

'Here was a woman who had pledged to spend her life helping the world's sick and damaged people, and who was yearning for the partner who could share that life. She could see this man as the man she was looking for. It was his devotion to the sick and his skills in operating. She needed somebody that would link her with humanity, and I feel that she thought he would be her life partner and that he would help her on her mission of love.'

Hasnat Khan was a thirty-six-year-old heart surgeon from Pakistan who had arrived at the Brompton in 1992 to work alongside arguably the world's number one heart specialist at the time, Professor Sir Magdi Yacoub, and to study for his PhD.

Over the course of her visits to Joseph, Diana was to have a few more encounters with Hasnat Khan. She told Simone Simmons that the first time she and Khan were alone was in a lift at the Royal Brompton Hospital, after one of her visits to Joseph.

She admitted to Simone that Khan was not her type at all, that he was overweight, that he smoked and ate the wrong food, but she was convinced that her meeting him had been 'karmic'. Almost from the start she felt her destiny lay with Hasnat Khan.

11
'Natty'

The first thing that strikes you about Hasnat Khan is his eyes. He has been compared to Omar Sharif, and described as 'the dishy doctor', but to do this is to miss the point. Instantly you sense here is a man of great compassion. His bearing is modest and unassuming, but his eyes seem to burn fiercely with his desire to care for the sick and diminish human suffering.

This is what those who describe Khan as a 'great man' mean. Diana must have sensed these things, too.

Khan is a man of little formality with no airs and graces. Quite often he would dress in Bermuda shorts if he was in Diana's company, and he is the kind of man who never has food in the fridge.

The living room of his one-bedroom bachelor flat in Chelsea reflects his tastes and lifestyle. All around are medical volumes, travel books and jazz CDs. A bottle of Coke sits next to his computer on the desktop.

Takeaways form the backbone of his diet, and he makes regular trips to his favourite place on the corner of the Cromwell Road, in South Kensington. Instant coffee and cigarettes fill in for the rest.

'Natty', as his family affectionately calls him, is described by his relatives as a very warm person, but the type who can't say no and likes to please, saying he'll do something even if he might not be able to.

Although he has lived abroad he is a traditionalist and believes in the importance of decency, honesty, hard work and family values. His dedication to his work is unquestioned; his career comes first.

His kindness and generosity are alluded to by affectionate tales from his cousin Mumraiz who remembers liking a pair of shoes Hasnat was once wearing when he visited Pakistan recently to see his family. Within days of returning to London Hasnat had sent his cousin a pair of identical shoes. In addition when Mumraiz had lost his wallet once and couldn't buy himself a computer game he'd been saving for, Hasnat drew out fifty pounds from the cash point and gave it to him.

He's been described as very lively, good fun to be around, with a strong sense of humour.

The relationship with his parents is close. He does not like to do anything that will annoy them, and he has never demanded anything from them. His mother is a very strong-willed individual, and Hasnat Khan always listens to what she has to say.

Hasnat Khan was born into a very wealthy middle-class family in August 1959, the oldest child in a family of four. His father, Rasheed Khan, together with Rasheed's older brother Said, established a highly successful glass business, called 'Prime Glass', which produced everyday glassware and bottles for the whole of Pakistan.

The factory premises formed part of a private estate situated about three miles outside the city of Jhelum, 195 kilometres north of Lahore. At the time of Hasnat's birth the family lived on the estate.

Behind the walls, secluded amongst huge gardens and vast orchards, were two large houses known in turn as the 'Big House' and the 'Little House'. The 'Big House' was where Hasnat's uncle Said and his family of eight children lived, and the 'Little House' was where Hasnat Khan himself grew up, with his smaller family of two sisters and a brother.

Diana pictured in September 1995 – the month she met Hasnat Khan.

A kiss for the cameras – the world believed in a fairytale wedding in July 1981.

Ten years later at the Gulf forces victory parade the cracks in the marriage
are visible even in public.

Professor Akbar Ahmed lecturing on Islam at the Royal Anthropological Institute. Diana hears there's 'a place for women and women are loved' in this religion.

Diana with Lady Elsa Bowker (centre) who says she became the go-between in Diana's relationship with Oliver Hoare.

Reading up on Islam during a skiing holiday at Lech in Austria, April 1994.

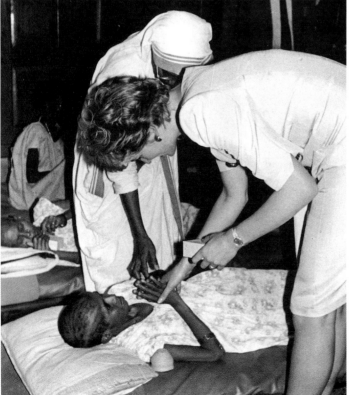

Diana in Pakistan in 1991 with her consort Abida Hussain. The Princess expressed a desire to meet a man who combined elements of the East and the West.

Handing out sweets at Mother Teresa's hospice for the dying in Calcutta, February 1992.

Diana poses alone in front of the world's greatest monument to love.

With the Missionaries of Charity in Calcutta where Diana spoke of a feeling that she had her own mission to be fulfilled.

Oliver Hoare, dealer in Islamic art.

Diana with her close friend Roberto Devorik attending a London film premiere

Pictured with designer Rizwan Beyg wearing the traditional Pakistani shalwar kameez he had made for her.

Wearing the same shalwar kameez on the day Prince Charles's lawyers announced details of the divorce settlement.

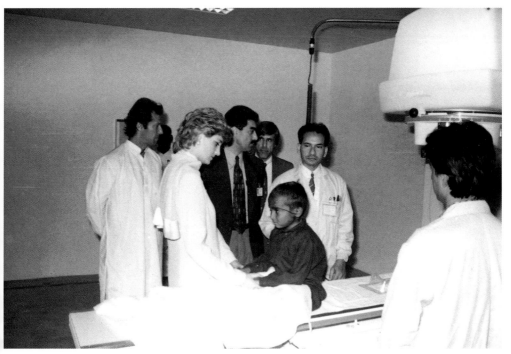

With Ashraf Mohammed as he prepares to undergo a brain scan at Imran Khan's cancer hospital in Lahore.

Diana cradles Ashraf while attending a show performed by children with cancer along with Jemima Khan and Annabel Goldsmith.

Attending a fund raising banquet in Lahore with Imran Khan. She confided in the former cricketer turned politician, and told him of her secret desire to marry Hasnat Khan.

With Imran and Jemima Khan. Diana looked to the Khans' marriage as a model for what she wanted for herself.

The contrast with Diana's childhood is a stark one. Although both families were wealthy, Diana's upbringing was quite formal, with the children being segregated from the parents. There was an 'upstairs, downstairs' factor which often prevented Park House feeling like a warm, family home.

Diana was six when her mother left home and, even by the age of nine, she had still not joined her father in the dining room for a meal; he was a loved but somewhat remote figure. The atmosphere was hardly natural or relaxed. By contrast, Hasnat Khan grew up in the certain knowledge and security that he was cared for and loved. The closeness of his own family and that of his uncle meant there were always many adults on hand to look after the children and spend time with them. It was a solid stable environment.

The children from the two houses, both 'Big' and 'Little', along with several of their cousins who would come and stay during school holidays, would constantly be playing hide and seek and climbing the trees in the vast orchards surrounding their home.

Their young imaginations would run riot with the fantasies and imaginings of a childish world of battles and conquests between good and evil. Stories would be woven about evil snakes that lurked in the depths of the orchard, which in their minds became a forest. The snakes would devour all in their path until being slain by the victorious knights – the children, of course – who rescued all the people from terror.

On lazy afternoons, long railway trains would be constructed from upturned chairs that had been hauled from the houses. Climbing inside, the children would set off on magical adventures across the globe – crossing the highest mountains, spanning the deepest gorges, and marvelling at all the sights along the way.

As the family estate was on the outskirts of the city of Jhelum, young Hasnat Khan had to travel some distance to school, but these trips seemed to have their own magic about them as well. Journeys on the cold mornings of the winter months would be made in a 'Tonga', the name given to a horse-drawn carriage.

The three-mile ride to the Convent school in Jhelum was bitterly cold and the children, huddled under blankets, would blow the mist out of their mouths and pretend to be smoking.

Landmarks along the way, such as an old colonial statue, formed the basis of good-natured games, and it became a competition to see who could spot them first. These were happy childhood days.

At school Hasnat was well behaved, and liked both by teachers and pupils. He is remembered as being jolly and droll; there was a spark in his stories, which he would relate in a very artistic way. Academically he proved to be extremely bright.

He remained in Jhelum until he had finished his A levels, and after that he left his home town and spent five years studying at the King Edward Medical College in Lahore. An imposing building fronted with white pillars, it is the main college for medicine in the Punjab, and one of the oldest established in Pakistan.

His initial studies over, Khan left his country for Australia where his uncle, Professor Jawad Khan, also an eminent heart surgeon, had arranged a position for him through his professional contacts.

At St Vincent's Hospital in Sydney, he met his first medical mentor Victor Chang, a much respected and admired cardiac specialist.

Dr Chang was a man of vision, an original thinker whose personal dream was to see a team of world-class researchers based at St Vincent's. He saw the field of heart disease as posing unique challenges and he advocated increased research and the development of various cardio-thoracic devices. These included an artificial heart valve and an artificial heart.

Khan saw Chang as a father figure, but on 4 July 1991, tragedy struck. Chang was driving to work in his blue Mercedes-Benz when he was forced off the road. It was part of a plot to extort three million Australian dollars from the heart surgeon by two Malaysian-born crooks.

Rather than submit to threats when one of them produced a

gun, Dr Chang argued with his two assailants. He shouted out to passers-by to call the police.

When Dr Chang refused to get into the kidnappers' car, the gunman fired, hitting the heart specialist in the cheek. As Chang lay helpless, he fired again. The shot penetrated Dr Chang's brain, killing him instantly.

The death of his mentor shattered Hasnat Khan, and shortly afterwards he decided to leave Australia and move to England.

In 1992 Khan went to live in Stratford-upon-Avon, moving to jobs in hospitals in Manchester, Leeds and Hammersmith, London, before ending up at the Royal Brompton. It was there on 1 September 1995 that Diana, then thirty-four years old, met the man who was to shape her future.

Part Three
The Doctor

12

'He's doing everything he tells his patients not to do!'

'What do you think?'

The woman did a twirl in her sitting room, and the onlooker was 'gobsmacked'.

'It's me!' said Diana.

She was wearing a long dark brown wig recently acquired on her behalf by her butler Paul Burrell from the Oxford Street department store, Selfridges.

Simone Simmons was silenced. Diana's image was totally transformed, fooling even those closest to her. It was one of several wigs Diana had had adapted for herself, and such disguises became the key to going out with Khan, safe from detection by public and paparazzi alike.

It also gave the Princess a chance to experience what other people take for granted in a normal relationship.

As well as hiding her blonde hair with the wig, Diana adjusted her make-up with appropriate matching shades, rather than the blues and pinks she would ordinarily wear to go with her natural colouring. She also changed her usual style of clothes, opting instead for leggings and trainers. Sometimes she even wore glasses with clear glass instead of lenses, to make absolutely sure that no one would recognize her.

For the seventeen days during which Joseph Toffolo had lain in bed recovering from his ordeal, Diana had visited the hospital every day, sometimes in casual clothes, at other times on her way to or from a social or official engagement and dressed accordingly.

During her early visits Diana would pull up a chair to Joseph's bedside, simply holding his hand and providing a comforting presence. When Joseph started to feel stronger she would give him a quick embrace the moment she entered the room. On these visits she would rarely turn up empty-handed. As well as bringing such universal hospital visiting gifts as grapes and flowers, she would sometimes arrive clutching books and records, including a set of three CDs by the Italian tenor Luciano Pavarotti, who was another of her friends. Toffolo himself admitted to being surprised at all the attention he was receiving.

In his room, Diana would behave in a totally natural way, laughing, joking and conversing with Joseph's other visitors. Sometimes things would get out of hand. On one occasion the atmosphere grew so boisterous that Joseph kicked them all out. As he gained more strength, Diana would walk with him along the hospital corridors, insisting that he lean on her arm while they quietly chatted together.

On 3 September Diana wrote to thank Oonagh for allowing her to be at Joseph's bedside at such an intimate moment, saying she felt enormously touched to be included into her family.

It was during this time that Diana started to get to know Hasnat Khan. She told him she wanted to understand how the hospital was run, and he acted as her willing guide.

He started introducing her to other patients, and he would accompany Diana on secret late-night visits to the hospital, escorting her out of the building through a back door.

On 20 November, eleven weeks after Diana's first encounter with Hasnat Khan, the controversial *Panorama* interview with Martin Bashir was aired. She had been discussing the terms of a wide-ranging interview with Bashir since late September, and it was agreed to tape on 5 November, Guy Fawkes Day, when her staff were away from Kensington Palace. During the interview Diana was asked whether she thought she would ever be queen. She expressed a wish to have a clearly defined role, and become, in a phrase which has since been used to define her, 'queen of people's hearts'.

On 30 November, ten days later, she was spotted by a *News of the World* photographer leaving the Brompton some time after midnight. Just as the photographer was taking the pictures, the paper's Royal editor Clive Goodman called him on his mobile and the Princess asked to speak to him. She told Goodman she was making regular visits to comfort the sick and the dying in hospital. She let it be known that two or three times a week she sat at the bedside of patients who are terminally ill, and who have no friends or relatives to offer support. The patients, with whom she spent up to four hours a night, needed someone to talk to, she said, and although some would live and some would die, they all needed love while they were in hospital. She explained that as well as just trying to be there for the patients, she actually drew strength from them. While it is true Diana did visit these patients, and grew close to some of them, it seems reasonable to suppose that she was further motivated by her desire to see Hasnat Khan.

All of Hasnat and Diana's initial meetings had taken place inside the Royal Brompton Hospital whilst her friend Joseph Toffolo was convalescing. But Diana thought it was time to invite him into her territory. And so she asked him to Kensington Palace for dinner, ostensibly to talk about heart surgery – she wanted to know 'all about it'.

They began to see each other more frequently but if the relationship was to lead anywhere, they couldn't just hide inside the hospital or the Palace.

Diana was determined to keep her relationship as quiet as possible, but still find a way to go out with him in public and behave as a normal couple. Hence her adoption of the intricate disguises.

They worked. Hasnat has a passion for jazz, and Ronnie Scott's in London's Soho became a favourite haunt for the couple, and the scene for some of their most enjoyable evenings out together.

Although she was a lover of music, Diana had never really explored the world of jazz. She rang Simone Simmons for advice about what she should listen to and, acting on the advice, she went out and bought CDs of Ella Fitzgerald, Louis Armstrong and Dave Brubeck.

Diana described the music on the discs as 'interesting'. But she found the experience of going to a jazz club to be wholly novel. The first time, she was so excited that she called Simone from outside Ronnie Scott's, just to say how much she loved standing in the queue. She admitted she had never had to stand in line for anything in her life before. 'I'm queuing!' she said, 'It's wonderful – you meet so many different people in a queue!'

Whilst Hasnat had gone up to the entrance to ask the door-men what the likelihood was of getting in, and how much longer they would have to wait, Diana had been busy chatting to people in the queue, and recounting her experiences to Simone, practically as they were happening.

Although trying not to burst the bubble, Simone pointedly said that she had to queue at the supermarket every day and quite honestly couldn't see the attraction, but Diana was ecstatic; she felt involved in the real world.

The Princess was in one of her disguises: leggings, a bomber jacket and a pair of glasses with plain lenses. Even in disguise, however, Diana presented an attractive image. She once phoned up Simone and explained how she had been standing in the fore-court of a tube station where two 'chaps' were deep in conversation. But as she walked past they both looked up distractedly, and Diana distinctly heard one of them say to the other 'I'd like to give her one!' It's the sort of comment that many women might find threatening, but Diana was tickled pink, saying, 'Can you imagine if they knew whom they were talking about!'

Diana and Hasnat enjoyed dining out in restaurants, or sometimes just nipping down to the 'chippy' for some cod and chips.

By all accounts Hasnat Khan was not the most health conscious of people. Certainly his job didn't leave him much spare time to shop and cook, so he grew accustomed to living off take-aways. Simmons says, 'Sometimes Diana would be on the phone to me and she would say, "I can see him walking down the road now with a bag of fried chicken", and she would start giggling and then say, "I can't believe it, it smells disgusting that stuff." She said to me, "He's a heart surgeon and he's doing everything he tells his patients not to do. He eats fatty foods, he smokes too much and he drinks too much!"'

During this time, Diana physically bloomed. According to a close friend she had a 'wicked sparkle' in her eyes. Her skin took on a glow and she gave the appearance of walking on air.

She called Hasnat 'Mr Wonderful'.

To the amazement of many, Diana even honed her cooking skills and learned how to use the microwave. She once boasted proudly to Simone that she'd cooked pasta for Hasnat. Simmons told her, 'I can't believe it; you actually cooked pasta?' Diana nodded, 'Yes, I learned how to use the microwave. Marks & Spencer have got these very clever little meals that you just put in the microwave and you put the timer on and press the button and it's done for you!"'

That was Diana's idea of cooking a meal, but simple as it may have been along any scale of culinary invention, her pride in the finished product was unsurpassed.

Extra ashtrays were dotted around Kensington Palace for Hasnat Khan to smoke. Diana said it was a good job that 'Fergie' had cigarettes so she had the ashtrays at the ready!

Diana knew exactly how best to avoid the press and keep the relationship secret. If she went to pick up Khan, a journey that would normally take about ten minutes by car across London, she would drive around for as long as forty minutes to avoid anyone tailing her, before venturing anywhere near her final destination.

Diana would use a variety of cars: her own, her butler's or a Range Rover. She would drive over to the Brompton Hospital, pick Hasnat up, and then return with him on the back seat covered over by a blanket.

Later on Diana would sometimes go over to the Harefield Hospital in Middlesex if Hasnat was working there, leaving the premises in the early hours of the morning.

Khan himself did not place much importance on the car he drove. Diana told Simmons about one time when Khan wanted to pick her up. She said, 'I don't think I could go in that car because the exhaust is falling off and it makes an awful lot of noise, and if we got stopped by the police I think they would have something to say about it, along with the rest of the world!' Diana once offered to buy Khan a new car, but he resolutely refused.

The staff at Kensington Palace were kept in the dark about what was going on. Even her trusted butler Paul Burrell was not made aware of the relationship until long after it was firmly established. If it was late in the evening when Hasnat turned up at the Palace she would be the one to let him in through the back door. If Hasnat stayed over at the weekend, she would simply ask Burrell to keep the other staff away and occupied in another part of the apartment until he had left.

Her staff were not the only ones she kept her new relationship from. Even some of those she considered to be her closest confidants were not told what was going on. Her friend Lady Elsa Bowker was to hear of it only by accident.

Lady Bowker had been invited to lunch with some friends at Boodle's, a London gentleman's club in St James's. There were seven people around the table including the former Belgian ambassador to London, the late Robert Vaes. As lunch was being served one of Lady Bowker's friends leaned across the table and said, 'Your friend, Elsa, is having an affair with a Pakistani.'

Lady Bowker was quite taken aback. 'I felt like saying, "People are talking stupidly." But I actually said, "Never, never." The friend replied, "I'm sure it's true." I said, "Never, never. Anyway I've never heard it." The Belgian ambassador said to me, "Elsa, why are you in a state of revolt? Do you know the Pakistani doctor?" I said, "No." "So how can you talk like this? He is the most wonderful man; a great gentleman, very intelligent, very kind and she'd be lucky if she had a man like him." I said, "Well, I'm amazed."'

According to her closest friends, the fact that Diana decided to keep her relationship with Khan so secret, even hiding it from many of her friends, is a reflection of how seriously she regarded it.

Roberto Devorik says they spoke about other relationships 'in an easier way than this one', and it was the fact that Diana wanted things kept secret that told him it was meaningful. 'With other relationships Diana would giggle when she spoke about them, and I would say, "They're good-looking" or "You must be having fun." But with Khan it was as if she wanted to protect him. I asked her about him, but she wanted to keep things private, and I said, "Bingo, this is a serious matter."'

When Devorik arrived at Kensington Palace on one occasion he passed through the gates and was asked to wait in the car for a while, before receiving clearance to go inside. Paul Burrell asked him, 'Roberto, are you sure you are expected today?' Devorik replied that Diana had definitely invited him to tea. Then Diana came out, and said, 'Roberto, you were supposed to come tomorrow.' He said, 'Oh, God, well, now I'm here I love your cucumber sandwiches, please let me stay – we have something to discuss.' She replied, 'Well, OK, but someone's coming to see me for a charity in one hour, and when the people arrive I'm going to see them downstairs, and you will have to leave.'

Looking back, Devorik says, 'It was somebody else who was coming to see her. She made me go, she never introduced me to him.'

Another night, Devorik was picking up a friend of his from a hotel in Knightsbridge, and the friend said, 'I think I saw your friend the Princess of Wales coming into the hotel.' 'Are you sure?' 'Yes, yes.' Devorik probed Diana in a later conversation saying, ' I caught you, Diana! I want to know who you were staying in the hotel with!' She told him that she had rented a private dining room at the hotel to give a dinner for the doctor and some friends from Pakistan. She was not giving it in the Palace because she wanted to keep it totally private.

Devorik is not alone in expressing the feeling that 'in a funny way I felt betrayed', despite all the things they had shared together – all the travelling, all the desperate phone calls at all kinds of unusual hours; this matter was something she hadn't shared with him.

Diana had admitted to her friend Simone Simmons that she didn't know why she was so attracted to Khan, but in truth Diana admired him enormously. He was a very different man to those she had met before. She thought he was a genius as far as heart surgery is concerned. And certainly she wasn't alone in her admiration of him.

Diana was developing an increasingly strong bond with Hasnat Khan the doctor. Yet this was by no means the only side of his life that appealed to her, or attracted her further research and inquiry. Eventually her thoughts began to revolve around Khan's large and close-knit family, over in Pakistan.

Estranged from the Royal Family, and often at odds with her own, Diana gravitated towards substitute families. She was a frequent visitor to the home of Hasnat's boss, Professor Sir Magdi Yacoub, and felt herself part of the family there. She also felt at home with Lady Annabel Goldsmith's family. Her daughter was Jemima Khan with whom Diana would talk about marriage to a man from the East. Lady Goldsmith recalls how Diana was a regular visitor to Ormeley Lodge in Ham Common, near London's Richmond Park, for either Saturday or Sunday lunch. 'Sunday lunch at Ormeley is usually chaotic. Everyone helps themselves, and lunch is eaten so fast that Diana eventually started to time us. "Right," she would say, "today was an all-time record – fifteen minutes." Laughter would ring round the table and everyone would speak at once. No ceremony here, and Diana loved it. She would drive down, usually managing to shake off the press, dash through the back door, greet the staff, try to evade the mass of dogs yapping at her feet, and settle down to amuse us. Certainly her repartee became an essential ingredient of these Sunday lunches. After coffee she would often offer to take the cups out to the kitchen – and just as often, I would find her there doing the washing up.'[1]

Diana's search for a family she could belong to and call her own, one that would make her feel loved and wanted was now about to bring her to the aristocratic clan of the Pathans.

1 *Requiem: Diana Princess of Wales 1961–1997*

13

'I'm sure we've met before'

Aworld away from the bustling and heavily polluted metropolis of the modern city of Lahore in Pakistan, is the district known as Model Town, the equivalent perhaps of Chelsea in London. Its quiet, wide streets are lined with palm trees, between which there are glimpses of palatial houses, often with two or three storeys, grand balconies and extensive grounds.

The families who inhabit this area are amongst the wealthiest, most privileged, best educated, and most powerful in the country. The district is home to doctors, writers, lawyers, teachers and politicians, and the former Prime Minister Nawaz Sharif had his house here before being jailed for life on terrorism and kidnapping charges.

Just off one of the busier roads, thick wrought-iron gates sweep open to reveal an imposing yellow-stone colonial house where children are enthusiastically playing cricket on the front lawn. This is the home of the Khan family.

A fan wheezes in one corner of the room and the muslin drapes waft gently in the cloying sultry heat of the early afternoon. The tiled floors are bare but for the odd scattered rug. The walls are whitewashed, and in the middle of the floor an old woman is kneeling as she recites her prayers.

Her name is Nanny Appa and she was born on 13 January 1911 in Ferozepur in what is now India. In 1947, soon after the partition of India and Pakistan, she and her husband moved to Lahore where they took over the three-storey colonial house in Model Town.

Appa gave birth to eight children: her daughter, Naheed, is Hasnat's mother.

The house itself is an imposing mansion with vast rooms and high ceilings. It echoes, as it surely has always done, to the sound of children's voices. Three generations live here.

In the summer months, the ceiling fans struggle to maintain something akin to a breeze in temperatures that regularly soar over a hundred degrees, a situation not helped by the frequent power cuts. In winter, by contrast, temperatures in Lahore can plummet to below zero. Most old houses in Pakistan never had central heating installed, making them bitterly cold. The tiled floors are icy, the high ceilings drawing up any lingering trace of warmth. But Nanny Appa doesn't feel the cold. Despite her eighty-nine years, she is the only one in the house who does not ask for a blanket or heater in winter. In fact she will open a window to let the fresh cold air in, chiding the young ones for their softness.

Although in theory the household employs servants to take care of regular chores such as cooking, cleaning and washing, if you peer into the kitchen before mealtimes, you will inevitably find Nanny Appa peeling the carrots herself, and often making her own meals. Naturally she will eschew any modern-day methods or gadgets. She takes comfort in the old ways.

Nanny Appa imbues the house in Model Town with its sense of stability and warmth. She defines the house, making it a haven of old-fashioned values, a quiet idyll where you will find generosity and compassion in good measure.

As she finishes her prayers now, she sighs heavily. No doubt she thinks of Diana, the woman she considered to be her adopted daughter, whom she prays for every day.

In the corner of one of the spare rooms lies an old wooden wardrobe. As Appa moves towards it her mood is heavy. Inside on the right are three shelves, and Appa tells you this is the place where she keeps all her special tokens from her past. Amongst the mementoes and keepsakes of a life's journey are two Jiffy bags containing letters and cards. As she takes them out she handles them with the respect that might be shown to holy relics. She points out there are very few things in the cupboard, but these, she says, are 'very special. She was my own!'

Back in her room Appa lays the contents of the Jiffy bags out on her bed, alongside a silver bowl and some perfumed candles. Such a display is given only to privileged visitors, for to her these letters, cards and gifts are sacred memories of a cherished loved one.

Even now, almost three years after Diana's death, Appa's emotions run very close to the surface when she thinks about the Princess. As she looks over the cards, one a painting by Claude Monet, 'White Nenuphars' – a bridge over water, the other a painting by Sir Lawrence Alma-Tadema, tears well up in her eyes, and begin to roll down her cheeks. 'My precious one is gone,' she says, 'and it makes me so sad.'

It was through Appa that the family received their first clue that there was a relationship between Hasnat and Diana, and it came in the form of a Christmas card. The bond between Nanny Appa and Hasnat Khan has always been a close one. Nanny Appa had cared for Hasnat when he was a small child, taking it in turns with his mother to breastfeed him. When Hasnat told Diana about his grandmother, she decided to send Appa a Christmas card. It was December 1995, and when the card – a picture of Diana and her two boys wishing Appa a Happy Christmas and a Happy New Year – arrived, the family admitted to being completely mystified. The card had arrived totally out of the blue, and was a surprise to them all. Members of the family each had their own theory, and they would exchange thoughts about how on earth Diana could possibly have known about Appa.

One of the theories was that it must be part of some kind of scheme whereby old age pensioners around the world were sent well-meaning seasonal wishes, and therefore Appa must be on the list!

It was only later that the family came to understand the significance of the card.

Over the next two years Diana was to develop an incredibly strong bond with Nanny Appa, through writing letters, exchanging gifts, sending flowers and visiting each other whenever the opportunity arose. Diana would tell Appa what was happening at Kensington Palace, what her children were doing, and how their education was coming along. She would often refer to her charity work, and to her need to care for the less fortunate around the globe. The letters were either written inside the cards or on informal notepaper. They were simple, friendly notes, such as a daughter would write to her mother.

The letters, all handwritten, chart the increasing closeness Diana felt to everyone in the Khan family. In the early days, not long after she had met the surgeon, Diana would say that she often thought about the rest of Hasnat's family, and that she was very keen to meet them all, but that would depend on whether and when he would allow her to.

Later, after she had finally got to know other members of the family, the letters would express her joy at the time she was able to spend with them, and her delight over the generous presents she received from them, such as a table and some china – both of which she evidently adored but felt she didn't deserve. Always she would extend to Appa her deepest love.

The exchange of letters and gifts was to continue for the rest of Diana's life and slowly Nanny Appa began to grow as fond of Diana as if she were one of her own daughters. Her gifts to the Princess were usually homely and personal items such as a yellow shalwar kameez or a shawl.

Diana also had historical connections to the Khan family, though she did not realize it at first. She had met one of Hasnat's uncles, Professor Jawad Khan, also a heart surgeon, by a remarkable coincidence in 1979.

Not far away from Model Town is a white two-storey building which houses the Pakistan Institute of Cardiology. Outside, the parking lot is piled high with rubble, a common sight in many Asian cities in their rush to become Westernized. But the pot-holes and the roadworks are a sign that things are already falling apart before they are even finished as the money has dried up or been siphoned off elsewhere.

Inside the hospital the corridors are thronging with people; the waiting rooms are bursting. This is one of Pakistan's largest centres of heart surgery, and two flights up is the office of its head surgeon, Professor Jawad Khan.

Jawad is Appa's second eldest son, and another member of the Khan family with whom Diana was to forge close links. Inside his office he examines an X-ray picture of a fourteen-year-old boy with a heart the size of a football. A registrar rushes in with the news that a patient who has not long left the operating theatre has developed complications; three other surgeons are waiting to see him to discuss working hours and role responsibility in theatre, and the phone rings constantly.

Jawad Khan faces you with the world-weariness of a man who knows his task is impossible. He is dealing with twelve to fifteen hundred cases a year, an average of thirty a week, but the resources are woeful, the equipment outdated; successive changes of government have left the health service crippled. Yet Khan's dedication to his profession and to his country is absolute, so there is an acceptance of the inevitable and a resolute determination to make the best of a bad job.

Mention Diana to him, and his eyes light up with a playfulness and sense of pride that transports him away from his immediate surroundings, and the stresses and strains of his profession are momentarily forgotten. His voice is instantly animated and he takes on the air of a storyteller who is about to impart something magical.

It was Professor Jawad, not Doctor Hasnat, who was actually the first member of the Khan family to meet Diana, he proudly tells you, at the very same hospital where she was to meet Hasnat some seventeen years later. The irony is not lost on the Professor as he recounts his story.

In the late 1970s Jawad Khan was a houseman training under Professor Sir Magdi Yacoub; like his nephew after him, he was based at the Royal Brompton Hospital in South Kensington. In September 1978 Diana Spencer's father, then fifty-four years of age, had collapsed with a massive brain haemorrhage. Diana was seventeen at the time.

Earl Spencer lay in a coma for several months and Diana's stepmother, Raine, former Countess of Dartmouth, supervised his care at the National Hospital for Central Nervous Diseases in central London. Two months later, when Earl Spencer suffered a relapse, he was moved to the Royal Brompton. He stayed there from November 1978 until January 1979.

Jawad Khan remembers the two young women who would sit in the waiting room. They came diligently every day and sat quietly for several hours at a time. He eventually discovered that the young visitors were the elder of Diana's two sisters, Jane, and Diana herself.

Jane was the spokeswoman for the pair; she would often ask how their father was and Khan would try to find out whatever information he could. He could see that Diana was just too upset to ask any questions; she left it to her sister, but always listened intently to the answers.

The second time he met Diana was again quite coincidental. This was the occasion of Diana's solo trip to Pakistan in September 1991, when she was being escorted by Seyeda Abida Hussain on her five-day official visit.

On 26 September Professor Jawad Khan was standing in a line-up of medical professors from Lahore's King Edward Medical College, waiting to be presented to the Royal visitor. Diana walked along the line, politely shaking everyone's hand in turn, sometimes asking a simple question. But when she reached Professor Khan, she came to a dead halt in front of him and said, 'I'm sure we've met before.'

Khan was quite taken by surprise and said simply, 'Yes, Ma'am, we met when your father was ill.' He was astonished that she should remember his face after thirteen years.

Little did Diana know then that just four years later she would fall in love with this man's nephew, and find herself back at the Royal Brompton Hospital – not waiting timidly, but visiting patients and observing heart operations.

Hasnat Khan has several relatives living in Britain. Among those he is extremely close to is his Uncle Omar, another of Appa's sons, and his aunt Jane, an English lawyer. At the time Diana knew them, Omar and Jane lived in Stratford-upon-Avon. Diana was keeping her relationship with Hasnat a secret from even some of her closest friends, but she and Hasnat were often able to spend time together at Omar and Jane's, and Diana developed her own close friendship with them as time went by. She liked the simple informality of the place, and the fact that for a time she was able to escape the pressures of her existence, and imagine herself to be part of an extended family.

As well as immersing herself in an entirely different culture, Diana was consistently interested in women who had made the transition across the cultural divide between East and West.

Jane, Omar's wife, had married into the Khan clan some years earlier, and being English she had had to go out to Lahore and face a family grilling over the question of her marriage to one of their own. Diana's attention was also being drawn to Jemima Khan who six months before had married the famous cricketer, Imran Khan.

According to another of Hasnat's uncles, Ashfaq Ahmed, brother of Nanny Appa and a well-known playwright in Pakistan, Diana first met Omar and Jane when she went to their house with Hasnat to collect some of his heavy surgery books. Hasnat had taken the books there so that he could study for an examination; now he wanted to retrieve them. This was a weekend when Diana and Hasnat had planned to be together, but Hasnat told Diana it would be impossible to meet up with her as he really needed the books and had to go up to Stratford to fetch them. Diana said, 'All right, I'll come with you, and keep you company in the car!' When they arrived at Omar and Jane's house, introductions were made and tea was served.

Some hours later Hasnat said, 'We'd better be getting back.' Diana asked, 'What about your books? You've come all the way over here to take them back to London.'

He said, 'No, thinking about it, they're too heavy.' Diana offered to help, and so she went upstairs, and from the balcony called out, 'Oh, they really *are* heavy, but I tell you what, I'll keep on throwing them down, and you keep on catching them, just like bricklayers do.' One by one – there were fifteen in all – they were lowered down to Hasnat.

Diana was able to spend time relaxing at the Stratford-upon-Avon house. Just as in her own apartment she would soon be busying herself with the mundane, domestic chores that she so enjoyed. She would pick up the plates from the table and put them in the dishwasher and then just sit in front of the fire, have a good chat and watch TV. She felt comfortable with the members of Hasnat's family she had met, and a part of her life that had for so long been vacant was being slowly filled.

14

'I have finished my ironing. Would you like me to do yours?'

By early 1996, Diana was engaged in tying up the loose ends of her earlier life. In particular she was attempting to secure the best possible divorce settlement.

By now an end was in sight to her marriage to Charles. The Queen – three years almost to the day since the couple's formal separation had been made public – had written to Diana requesting a divorce. As she told her Prime Minister, an early divorce was 'in the best interests of the country'.

A process of alienation that had begun with the Morton book had been thoroughly completed with her *Panorama* interview on 20 November 1995.

Yet provoking a rapid divorce had not been Diana's intention at the time of that interview. She was convinced she could actually remain married to Charles, but in the context of newfound respect and independence. To her mind, this would be a better marriage, on her terms.

The bitter truth came as a severe body blow for the Princess, and Simone Simmons says Diana fell apart. 'She couldn't sleep at night and started taking very strong sleeping pills. She was constantly in tears.'

Isolated and alone, Diana had spent Christmas Day by herself in Kensington Palace, and on 27 December she set off for the exclusive K club on the Caribbean island of Barbuda. Her companion was her twenty-six-year-old personal assistant, Victoria Mendham. As a result of the *Panorama* interview Diana lost two of her loyal members of staff: first her press secretary, Geoffrey Crawford, who had resigned immediately after the interview had been aired, and then her private secretary, Patrick Jephson, who left in January 1996 after eight years of service. Diana was, in the eyes of some observers, perilously close to a breakdown.

The telephone was ringing in fashion designer Rizwan Beyg's shop in Karachi, southern Pakistan, at the beginning of 1996.

On the other end of the line was Jemima Khan, saying that Princess Diana was thinking about making a two-day visit to Pakistan, and it would be good, she suggested, if the designer could fly to Lahore, bringing with him some samples of his embroideries, so that the two of them could sketch out a few ideas for some dresses for the Princess.

Jemima told him that Diana was hoping to make a fundraising trip for the hospital, accompanied by Jemima's mother Lady Annabel Goldsmith.

Beyg had never designed anything for a Princess before and was excited by the prospect of the most famous woman in the world wearing his clothes.

He duly packed a bag containing some samples of his designs and a week later headed for Lahore.

Once there he met Jemima Khan and one of Imran Khan's sisters, Aleema. They talked at length about what kind of dress he should make, and together they settled on three outfits that Diana would be most likely to wear for the hospital visit: there would be one main outfit, and then a couple of others as an option, that would be more ethnic in silhouette and style in case she preferred those.

The outfits were all to be in pale classic shades with thread and pearl embroidery. Beyg had been studying her style carefully and thought Diana would most likely wear something tailored. He could see that Diana had been defining her sense of self through the individuality of the clothes she was choosing in those days.

'Fashion,' he says, 'represents individuality. In Pakistan, the ingredients are pretty much the same; basically fabric and embroidery, ornamentation or silhouette, but all clothes are a manifestation of the self.' Beyg felt that Diana was very clear about the style she was looking for. And the fact that she had shown herself willing to wear a shalwar kameez demonstrated that she was quite ready to encompass other ideas and cultures.

Beyg returned to Karachi equipped with the basic Royal measurements, as provided by Jemima. Nevertheless he prayed the outfits would fit when Diana eventually tried them on.

After much consideration of the precise style for the main outfit, Beyg decided to go for the achkan, an outfit that is traditionally worn by men at weddings. However, he would make it substantially softer and more feminine. The classic mandarin collar was abandoned for a half collar with a deep vee to accentuate the neck. The shade was to be pale ivory, and had to have pearls as Diana loved them. The whole outfit was to be embroidered. The trousers were to be a derivative of the classic shalwar, cut like a trouser but still retaining the basic pantaloon shape.

He and his team set to work to make the outfit. More than two hundred hours were spent on the embroidery alone, and the whole outfit took three weeks to complete. But by the time Diana arrived in Pakistan, the dress was ready.

Six weeks into the New Year, and the white and green private jet taxied along the runway at Lahore airport on 20 February 1996, coming to a halt outside the terminal building. Diana emerged with Lady Annabel Goldsmith, the wife of financier Sir James Goldsmith, and with Lady Cosima Somerset, Annabel's niece.

No one had slept on the flight. According to Lady Annabel it was because Diana had made everyone laugh so much. 'The jet had seats that unfolded into beds, but Diana had become so hysterical with laughter at trying to recline her seat that she managed to fall out of it.'

'It was like a dormitory farce,' said Cosima.[1]

The airport was bustling with newsmen and camera crews, although none of the coverage was allowed to be broadcast on Pakistan's state-controlled television and radio stations as Benazir Bhutto, who had once invited Diana to Pakistan herself, now saw the Princess's visit as an attempt by her political opponent Imran Khan to boost his own ambitions and to gain votes. Imran Khan had been repeatedly accusing Bhutto's government of corruption.

The cancer hospital, which Khan had founded in memory of his mother who had died from the disease, had experienced a series of unfortunate setbacks, and everyone involved hoped that Diana's visit would raise its profile and boost fundraising efforts.

Since this was a strictly private visit there was no official welcome at the airport, so Diana climbed into the back of the black Mercedes next to Annabel and Jemima, with Imran himself at the wheel, and together they made their way from the airport towards the city centre.

Despite Benazir Bhutto's media clampdown, the whole city was buzzing with the news of Diana's arrival. On the road from the airport Imran Khan says there was an incredible reaction to her from the people of Lahore. It took him completely by surprise, as it was very unusual for his countrymen to react in such an enthusiastic way towards celebrities. In fact, Khan says no other celebrity ever had the impact that Diana had during that visit to Pakistan. When he originally opened his hospital he invited four of the top Indian film stars – still popular in Pakistan despite the long-standing differences between the two countries. The film stars made a big stir, but absolutely nothing compared to the impact Princess Diana had.

1 *Requiem: Diana, Princess of Wales 1961–1997*

While in Lahore, Diana was staying at a four-bedroom, hacienda-style mansion owned by multi-millionaire business-man Jehangir Monnoo, a close friend of Imran Khan, who had made his fortune in textiles and farming. It is a lavishly deco-rated house at Shah Jamal, in the centre of Lahore's plush Shadman district, and stands alongside the canal bank.

The living room was crammed full of Eastern artefacts, paint-ings and carpets, and outside was the swimming pool with diving board, near to a conservatory housing a jacuzzi, steam bath and sauna. On Diana's bed the owner had placed a Snoopy cuddly toy, and a troll doll, which was wearing a little T-shirt emblazoned with the message 'aged to perfection'.

That afternoon, at around four o'clock, Rizwan Beyg arrived at the Monnoo house. As he made his way towards the entrance the clothes designer had to be chaperoned through rows of security as by now the paparazzi were out in full force. Many of them were perched in trees, trying to catch a glimpse of Diana.

When Beyg arrived, the Princess was sitting by the pool relax-ing after her journey, but Jemima told the designer she would go to fetch her. Ten minutes later Diana appeared. She looked closely at the ivory outfit with the seed pearls on it, and instant-aneously fell in love with it, amazed by the craftsmanship. She told him she thought the embroideries were incredible. She, Beyg and Jemima chatted animatedly about the workmanship, the designs and the colours, before Diana apologized and said that as she was so very jet-lagged, would he mind if she didn't try it on there and then.

Beyg was still a little concerned that it should fit her perfectly but he understood her need to have a nap after the long flight. As he was about to leave he asked for one favour: would the Princess mind posing for a photograph with him?

Diana readily agreed and he went to his car to get his camera. To his dismay he realized he had forgotten it. Diana said it wasn't a problem and she would be happy to wait if he wanted to find one from somewhere. Beyg hadn't been gone long, but when he returned complete with borrowed camera he found

Diana wearing the outfit he had designed for her; she had decided to try it on after all. She told him that if they were to be in a photograph together then it really should be in something he had designed.

A snapshot was duly taken and by then Diana had obviously woken up again. She asked Beyg to stay for a coffee, during which they spoke at length about fashion in general and what was happening in Pakistan to the craft.

Beyg contrasted fashion in his country with that of the West. He said that the catwalks of Lahore were not quite like those in Rome, London or New York, and that there were religious constraints on what was deemed to be appropriate for Pakistani women to wear. Nevertheless, there was great beauty in the traditional material and styles.

The outfit Diana wore for the first time on that February day in 1996 went on to be very widely photographed later that year when her divorce settlement was announced, and came to be imbued with a deeper significance.

In Lahore, the day after Beyg had delivered the outfit to her, Diana toured Imran Khan's fifteen-million-pound Shaukat Khanum Memorial Cancer Hospital. Every year there are about five hundred thousand new cancer cases in Pakistan, says Khan, and his hospital is the only specialized institution there is for treating the disease in the country.

It is an impressive place. Built on the outskirts of Lahore it is modern and clean, employs six hundred staff, and the treatment for the majority of patients, most of whom are extremely poor, is free. The hospital relies almost entirely on donations for its continued survival, and once or twice has found itself in dire straits. It is only through a continuous hard grind of staging events and conducting campaigns all year round that the necessary money can be raised. Without it, the rich would continue to go abroad for their treatment, but the poor would face a certain death sentence.

Diana moved from ward to ward, taking in all the faces of the sick children. She was obviously concerned by what she was seeing, and wanted to know what she could do to help. But just her presence was a tonic to everyone that day, and she was determined that no patient should miss seeing her.

Outside in the hospital grounds, a giant tent had been constructed, and after the tour many of the children queued to sit on Diana's lap or to shake her hand. It was here that Diana encountered a seven-year-old boy called Ashraf Mohammed. Ashraf was terminally ill with a brain tumour and doctors had given him only a few weeks to live.

Diana cradled Ashraf as she watched a show being put on by other child patients. Imran Khan recalls that the boy was in a terrible state; it was too much for some to bear, but Diana was undaunted. Khan says that Ashraf had a festering tumour and it smelt very bad. He could smell it himself from five feet away, where he was sitting with Jemima. But Diana held the boy for half an hour, apparently totally oblivious to his condition; he said it was as if she was holding her own child. Diana told Ashraf's mother that she would arrange for suitable treatment in whichever country had it available.

During that visit to Lahore, Khan sensed Diana's emotional vacuum. He could see that she was very lonely and very insecure; but he could also tell that there was 'a sort of wildness' about her, that she was 'a bit of a rebel'. 'There was a side to her that was clearly unfulfilled: her private side. She wasn't happy with her life, and she probably wanted a lot more security, more of a family. On the other side she was this completely compassionate woman giving so much to other people, especially the underprivileged, people in pain. This was so genuine in her, and that's why she had so much love and respect.'

Imran Khan attributes her popularity to the unique blend of her character. She was 'very attractive and glamorous, then she was a royal figure, then she had a hugely compassionate side to her'.

In Khan's view she was not at all affected by race, nationality, religion. 'She seemed to be above all that. It was this combination of ingredients that made her such a great figure.'

Eighteen months later, when news of Diana's death reached Ashraf's family, they avoided telling the boy at first. But inevitably the tragic news leaked out to him, through the other children in the family. He simply said that it was 'God's will'. These were the last words he uttered; he never spoke again after that.[2]

After Diana's hospital visit, she and the rest of the party returned to the Monnoo house to wash and dress and prepare for a fundraising banquet that same evening. The dinner for five hundred people was to mark the Muslim festival of Ramadan, but was also designed to raise further funds for the hospital.

As Diana and Lady Annabel Goldsmith were getting ready, the electricity and water both suddenly cut out, and Lady Annabel found herself having to shower under a trickle of water with the aid of a torch. As Lady Annabel wrote in *Requiem*, Diana managed to bathe, too, albeit with interruptions from the houseboy who kept appearing in her room with a copy of the Koran in one hand – a present for her – and a notepad and pen in the other; he wanted her autograph. She succeeded in charming everyone, including the servants at the house.

Diana had made herself very much at home, and during the power cut she chatted about what colour nail polish she was going to wear, and how she would like to buy some sandals from the local market.

Later when the electricity was restored Lady Annabel noticed strange banging noises emanating from the upstairs landing. Suddenly it stopped and Diana called down, 'I've finished my ironing. Would you like me to do yours?'

At the fundraising dinner that evening an announcement was made over the microphone that Diana would sign some autographs. In an instant hundreds of woman converged on

---

2 *Despite a media campaign in 1999 aimed at bringing Ashraf to England for treatment as Diana had wished, the boy never made it. He died in the last week of January 2000.*

the table where she was sitting and totally surrounded her. It made Diana laugh. 'Why don't *you* sign my name, it's not that difficult,' she told them.

Aside from the obvious impact she made in helping to raise funds for the hospital, Diana also had personal reasons for the visit. She had become close to Annabel Goldsmith's daughter Jemima. When Jemima had married Imran Khan, twenty-two years her senior, eight months earlier in June 1995, Diana was curious about the mechanics of the couple's relationship. It was a union that seemed to combine the freedom of the West and the spirituality of the East, in which she had expressed so much interest to Abida Hussain during her visit to Pakistan in 1991.

Jemima had made the successful transition from Western girl to Asian wife, despite initial opposition to the match both from those Britons who thought she was betraying her background and from Pakistanis who felt she had no right to lay claim to one of their heroes.

Far from being put off, Jemima seems – at least from the outside – to have integrated into Pakistani life. She has converted to Islam, had two sons, Sulaiman and Kasim, and has taught herself to speak Urdu. Along the way she has won the respect of a once sceptical Pakistani public.

As her own feelings for Hasnat Khan grew, Diana discussed with Jemima the good and the bad points of marrying into a different religion. Diana was captivated by the culture that Imran was steeped in. She loved the Pakistani tradition of the close-knit, extended family, the society which revolved around family life, and which allowed mothers and children to be together at all times. It seemed to her a welcome contrast to her old life inside the Royal Family, with what she felt to be its coldness and remoteness. Jemima was living with Imran's father and sisters and their husbands and children and has since written that she believes there are many lessons to be learned from such a traditional society. Chief amongst these she picks out the joint family system, in which all the relatives are combined in a community of completely interdependent individuals, each of whom has an important role, regardless of age and gender. Whereas in the West one leaves home in order to mature and grow up, in Pakistan the family system creates, in her view, a much more solid foundation for a person's development. Among the clearest victims of the Western approach, for her, are working mothers. She has nothing but sympathy for their lack of social benefits and the fact that many find themselves forced to send their children to day care centres. In Pakistan they would remain within the family environment. She is also impressed by the Pakistani practice of dealing with marital problems within the family, rather than resorting to marriage guidance counsellors.[3]

Diana would sit up until the early hours of the morning discussing Jemima's marriage, and it made Diana think in a new, deeper way about the man she had met at the Brompton Hospital. As ever, Diana thought beyond her immediate relationship and wanted to meet members of Hasnat's family. She spoke to Imran's sisters about it, and they called Professor Jawad Khan to pass on the message. Jawad was worried about the press attention her visit was attracting, but he spoke to Diana on the phone at length. She said she would like to come and see him, and that she also wanted to meet Hasnat's mother, Naheed Khan. He explained his reservations about the press, and it was decided to hold off from meeting for the time being . . .

3 *Mirror*, 25 November 1997

15

'We should invite Ms Bhutto for a special viewing!'

For four months after returning from Pakistan, Diana was to make few appearances in public. In June, however, she flew to Chicago to help raise money for a number of cancer charities. Throughout this period her relationship with Hasnat Khan was developing further.

Sometimes they saw each other every couple of days, sometimes it was every couple of weeks because his work commitments took over. Usually they met at Kensington Palace, but on the odd occasion Diana would see him at his flat in Chelsea. After one visit there she reported back to Simone Simmons about her impressions of the place. She said, 'It's the flat of a typical man, it needs cleaning.' There were a couple of old mouldy mugs because Hasnat was never there to do anything. Evidence of his work was everywhere, and Diana said it was 'knee deep in papers', and she was, 'having difficulty finding a spare bit of floor'. 'It would,' she said, 'make a good carpet for students.'

Hasnat's overwhelming passion was his work, and all his energies and emotions went into it. So much so that often it came before Diana, and she was sometimes superfluous to his needs. But if, on many levels, Diana and Hasnat Khan did not have much in common, and had experienced completely different lives, yet there was something there, which Diana's friends describe as a 'chemistry' between them. Khan was so different

from the men she had met before, not part of the British aris-
tocracy, but a man dedicated to his career, saving lives.

They would talk about the Muslim religion – Diana was
fascinated by the strict dietary laws of Islam – but more importantly each was concerned in their own way with helping people,
and according to friends a tremendous bond developed
between them because of this.

'They had a lot in common, dealing with life and death,'
Debbie Frank says. 'It was very exciting for her to meet somebody who was a professional. Heart surgery is a very important
thing, and the doctor is almost omnipotent in those circumstances, and they have a lot of power to make somebody live.
Diana's own heart was broken; Khan seemed to be the perfect
person to heal her and to encourage her interest in helping
other people to heal. He was self-sufficient, self-contained. He
didn't want her royalty, her position, her status; he wasn't
impressed by any of that. As a heart surgeon he has an
extremely stressful life, working long hours, often exhausted.
Yet he was very constant and seemed able to cope under pressure, and Diana was able to cope better under pressure herself
as a result of having Hasnat in her life.'

Khan's medical power fascinated Diana. 'He has the power
of life over death,' she told a close friend when recounting his
attributes, and she wanted to know everything about the
human heart, how it worked, how it functioned. To this end
she obtained a copy of *Gray's Anatomy*, the classic almanac of
the human body that is compulsory reading for every student
of medicine, but hardly light bedtime reading for anyone else.
But Diana applied herself to the task and surprised Khan with
the extent of her knowledge. Having already made regular
private visits to comfort patients at the Royal Brompton,
Professor Sir Magdi Yacoub asked her if she would be interested in watching an operation. Diana readily agreed; for one
thing, this would enable her to share in Khan's professional
life.

She became a frequent visitor to the operating theatre, once watching four operations in one day at London's Royal Marsden Hospital. Despite being warned by doctors that some of the sights might shock her, the Princess coped admirably. Diana told her friends she thought that heart operations were fascinating, and that she didn't feel at all squeamish.

On 23 April 1996 she was filmed by a camera crew from Sky News as she witnessed a heart operation at Harefield Hospital involving a seven-year-old African boy called Arnaud Wambo. Hasnat apparently helped her to 'scrub up' beforehand.

However, the presence of the television camera did her no favours at all; Diana received much criticism for her attendance at the operation, not just because she could have been a distracting influence, or for possibly getting in the way, but also because she was wearing mascara.

There was nothing superficial about Diana's interest, though. She was delving deep into the world of medicine in general and heart surgery in particular. This allowed her to understand Hasnat's professional world, so that the two of them would be able to discuss his work or his studies without all the detail going way above her head.

It also brought moments of humour. Once, when Hasnat was working at Northwick Park Hospital in Harrow, Middlesex, he felt dismayed. He had been practising heart operations on sheep all week, but all of his sheep had died. After the eleventh death he phoned Diana and told her what had happened. She was very sympathetic with him on the phone, and afterwards set about trying to cheer him up. In a typical example of Diana's playful sense of humour, her solution to the crisis was to buy him an inflatable sheep called Daisy. That way, she said, he could be sure to have at least one sheep to operate on.

For his part Khan was impressed by Diana's natural affinity with the sick, and her tireless efforts to offer comfort to them. He admired the way she would quite naturally sit by bedsides holding the hands of those recovering from the surgery performed by himself and his colleagues, and that she did this not for any reason of fame, but simply because she cared.

Diana and Hasnat were growing closer and closer, and the Princess increasingly confided in Khan, talking about the breakdown of her marriage, and the trauma of trying to reach a divorce settlement with Prince Charles. He was a solid support to her and someone she could lean on in times of need.

It was 4 July 1996, and the paparazzi were out in full force. Less than two hours earlier Prince Charles's lawyers had announced the divorce settlement which would end his marriage to Diana, and the call for which the Princess had been waiting since April had finally come through to her private apartment at Kensington Palace.

Diana learned she would receive a seventeen million pound lump sum, as well as more than four hundred thousand pounds a year for expenses connected to her official duties and her office.

Diana arrived at the Dorchester Hotel in London's Park Lane as guest of honour for a huge fundraising dinner that Imran Khan was holding for his cancer hospital. It was one of the most dazzling society events of the year attended by six hundred glitterati. She was at the centre of a pack of photographers.

She was wearing the outfit that had been designed for her in Lahore in February that year by Rizwan Beyg, the ivory pearl-studded shalwar kameez. Pictures of Diana dominated the late-evening television bulletins, as well as the world's news-papers the following morning. The outfit that was captured by a hundred lenses as she strode through the flashbulbs came to be symbolic of a breaking away from the institution of marriage, and from Royalty; it came to represent a form of liberation, an expression of her longed-for independence, and her passage from one rigidly controlled life into another which held untold mysteries.[1]

1 *The shalwar kameez is now on show in the museum of the Spencer Estate, at Althorp in Northamptonshire.*

On 12 July the final agreement of the divorce settlement was reached, and on 15 July Charles and Diana filed their 'decree nisi', the document declaring that the fifteen-year marriage would be officially dissolved on 28 August. Just one day after the decree nisi, Diana announced a massive restructuring of her outside responsibilities. She intended to resign as president or patron of more than a hundred diverse organizations, and instead devote more time to just six chosen charities.

As news of the divorce was announced on television, Hasnat Khan was sitting in the lounge at the house of his Uncle Omar and Aunt Jane in Stratford-upon-Avon watching the coverage. With him were Hasnat's grandmother Nanny Appa, and his young teenage cousin, Mumraiz, who had both flown over on a visit from Pakistan.

At around four o'clock in the afternoon Diana drew up at the house in her car, having driven up from London by herself. Hasnat introduced her to Mumraiz and finally to Nanny Appa. The two women had been corresponding for the last six months, and were delighted finally to make each other's acquaintance. Diana had been maintaining her links with Hasnat Khan's family as well as strengthening her relationship with the doctor.

Hasnat's cousin, Mumraiz, had come to England to play cricket. At thirteen, he was very close in age to Diana's two sons, and she had suggested to Mumraiz's father, Professor Jawad Khan, that he might like to join her and the boys on holiday.

After a cup of tea at Omar and Jane's, Diana said she fancied watching a movie. Mumraiz was dispatched to the local Blockbuster Video store, where he chose the second of the *Ace Ventura, Pet Detective* films, starring Jim Carey. Diana told Mumraiz that she had just taken her sons to see a similar movie for William's birthday.

They all sat and watched the video together; it was a simple family evening watching the television, laughing a lot and telling jokes.

After the film was over, Appa cooked dinner; dhal, rice and salad, and over the table Diana told the family about the poor state of health of Sir James Goldsmith, father of Jemima Khan. Goldsmith had been giving Diana behind-the-scenes help with her divorce settlement, and she had seen him just a few days earlier at the Dorchester Hotel gala for Imran Khan's cancer hospital.

As was becoming her habit, once they had all eaten Diana helped clear the table and do the washing up, finally leaving them quite late in the evening. Hasnat stayed in Stratford overnight, driving himself back to London the following day in his red Vauxhall Astra.

A couple of weeks later, at the beginning of August, the holiday was over and Nanny Appa and Mumraiz were due to return to Lahore. Before they left, Diana asked the family over for afternoon tea at Kensington Palace.

Things were behind schedule. Omar and Jane had loaded their car with Nanny Appa and Mumraiz's suitcases, ready to drive them on to Heathrow Airport for their flight back home immediately after they had finished tea. But traffic being what it is, the journey from Stratford had taken longer than planned, and they arrived late at the Palace. Having gone through the formalities at the gate, Diana was already downstairs waiting anxiously for them.

She took them through the palace corridors and staircases until they reached her 'little lounge' where they were to have tea.

Mumraiz was amazed at all the photographs of William and Harry. It seemed to him that the walls of the room were covered from top to bottom by pictures, with hardly an inch of space left over. It was some indication of her constant love and attachment to her boys.

Appa remembers thinking that the sitting room where they were was 'cosy' and that Diana's personality was reflected in everything around her. In that room, she felt that 'everything was nicely done', but her overall impression of Kensington Palace was that 'it was such a big place for Diana alone. It was very nice, but very lonely'.

Diana made some introductions. First of all she introduced the family to a Bengali who was Diana's Palace cook. Appa was anxious to know if the man spoke Urdu, but it turned out he didn't.

Afternoon tea arrived, wheeled in on a trolley filled with sandwiches and cakes. Diana hovered nervously on the edge of her seat, wanting everything to be all right, conscious no doubt that catering for friends wasn't perhaps her strongest point. For a while it looked as though a culinary disaster might be looming, as Nanny Appa, with a bemused expression on her face, lifted up the corners of several of the sandwiches. Diana wondered what was going on and asked Jane to translate. It seemed Appa was worried the sandwiches might contain ham, and being hard of hearing it took some time to persuade her they were in fact salmon! But once the potential disaster had been averted everyone had a good laugh.

The discussion turned to Hasnat. He had been invited along for tea but hadn't turned up. Word had come through that he was held up in the operating theatre, which was not uncommon for any doctor.

Jane and Diana were making fun of the Khan family saying they were always late, or didn't show up at all. The family admitted that lateness was a typical Pathan trait; they are generally not very punctual and always very laid back.

Diana said of Hasnat, 'He never sticks to time, and he is very noncommittal.'

Cakes were served, and then Diana presented Appa with a gift. Once again her nervousness was apparent as she watched the Khan matriarch unwinding the wrapping paper; she didn't want to do anything to offend her honoured guests.

Mumraiz was recording the event on the family's home video camera, and for once, Diana was relishing the opportunity to be on TV. She even cracked jokes saying, 'We should invite Ms Bhutto for a special viewing!'

Opening the box, Appa discovered a silver bowl, to the sounds of 'ooh's and 'aah's from the family. Appa stared in silence, lost for words. 'I took it out,' she recalls, 'it was made of pure silver. It was very heavy. That bowl is always going to be very special as

Diana looked for it, and packed it herself.' Today, the silver bowl is kept safe at the Khan house in Model Town in Lahore.

On 28 August 1996, once the divorce from Charles was finalized, the relationship with Hasnat entered a new plane. Diana had already told her close circle of friends of her plans to remarry once she was free of the House of Windsor.

Diana was becoming more self-contained as a result of her relationship with Hasnat and more patient. On a visit to her friend Lady Elsa Bowker, Diana said she was 'no longer lonely' and that she had 'found peace'. Hasnat had given Diana a photograph of himself for a Christmas present, and she kept it at her bedside. By the end of 1996 there was a picture of Hasnat's grandmother Appa next to the bed as well. These two photos sat alongside pictures of her children, and her own family. Diana had also asked Appa for a photograph of Hasnat and her together, saying she would keep it with her always.

Diana talked about becoming plain old 'Mrs Khan' with Simone Simmons, and admitted she wanted to have Khan's children, dreaming about living in a nice little cottage some-where. Diana arranged for her two sons to meet Hasnat so she could see what they thought of him. 'She told me that she spoke with the children about this special relationship,' says Roberto Devorik. 'Prince William said, "Mummy, you have to do what makes you happy."' Diana told her friend Simone Simmons that Hasnat was uneasy at being introduced to William and Harry, and Diana admitted she wasn't at all sure if he was ready to become stepfather to two very self-possessed adolescents.

She tried to persuade Hasnat to move into Kensington Palace, offering him the use of Charles's suite of rooms, so that he could even have an office there. Khan did not think this was a good idea at all, because then the relationship would have to go public. That was the last thing he wanted.

16

'We are laughing ourselves silly over this'

Diana undoubtedly had a love–hate relationship with the media, and the media in turn had an obsessive fascination with her.

The relationship bore an uncanny resemblance to the two main characters in the Tom and Jerry cartoons; one day they love each other, the next day they're doing their best to hide, or to attack each other.

Roberto Devorik describes an occasion when they were in Rome together, and Diana wanted to see the Trevi Fountain. The press were soon hot on their trail. 'The amount of little Vespa motorcycles following us was unbelievable, they were like bees, and what they did was really obnoxious. They would bang the windows of the car with the back of the camera, so it would sound like somebody was shooting. Immediately one would wind down the window to see what was going on, and then the picture would be taken. Obviously Diana knew the old trick, and she said, "That's what they're expecting you to do; don't do it, Roberto, don't do it." And I said, "What do you mean?" She said they want us to open the window to take the picture.'

Diana used to speak to her friends of the 'vultures', the predators who would pick away at her piece by piece. She always said that she found the press very intrusive and very invasive. She enjoyed her privacy but she rarely got any.

The moment she left the Palace she would have a stream of motorbikes and cars following her. If she wanted to take a walk in Kensington Palace Gardens other than at the crack of dawn, she knew that she would have crowds of them following her on foot. Wherever she went they would be waiting – whether it was outside the gym, the homes and offices of her therapists, or the houses of close friends – and in the end she became more secretive than may have been strictly necessary.

All she wanted was normality and a sense of balance. But there were no 'normal' moments in Diana's life. The press only heightened her sense of isolation. All the fun of going to see the Trevi Fountain, or merely going out shopping – something the rest of us take for granted – totally collapsed when she was being chased down the street, or having lenses poked in her face.

Diana's physical isolation was entirely due to her fame, but it created a bizarre and strangely contradictory type of loneliness, whereby she was constantly surrounded by thousands of photographers but actually felt herself to be totally alone.

Simone Simmons recalls Diana telephoning her from Italy from one of her mobile phones. Diana blurted out, 'Have you seen *Hello* magazine this week?' 'No,' said Simmons. 'Get it,' Diana urged.

Simmons tramped down the stairs of her apartment block, bought the magazine and called Italy. Diana said, 'Do you see what I mean? It's like "Spot the Diana". There was me and two thousand photographers, and it was an absolute nightmare!' All that could be seen in the photograph was a little head circled by thousands of people, graphically illustrating for Diana the contradiction of her lonely position.

Yet there were many ways in which Diana actually needed the press, subconsciously at first, but later on a conscious level as well.

At the subconscious level, her insecurity demanded the

presence of the press, however unwelcome they might have been, because they reinforced her sense of identity. In her loneliness they were practically the only constant she could rely on.

Mark Saunders, one of the so-called 'paparazzi' whose speciality is photographing the Royals, recalls how Diana would occasionally make her way over to him and his colleague Glen Harvey for a chat, just because she needed to talk with someone.

At the conscious level, within a decade of first being thrust into the merciless gaze of the public eye, Diana, like many celebrities, had become supremely skilled in manipulating the press for her own ends, initially by influencing what was written, and later by orchestrating the images as well, quite often without the photographers themselves being aware of it.

Editorially, she discovered the knack of controlling newspaper headlines. Usually she would do this by giving 'friendly' reporters stories that she wanted to be put in the papers. They would always contain the words 'A source close to the Princess said', when in reality the source was often Diana herself.

By contrast, Hasnat Khan was extremely uncomfortable with the press, almost pathologically so. 'He is an intensely private man who has never and will never enjoy being in the limelight,' says his aunt Maryam.

His family says that in any relationship, even if it be with his own friends, his idea of nirvana is to have a quiet evening in; he is really quite a loner in that sense.

Members of his family recall how certain photojournalists would sit literally for days on end outside Khan's Chelsea flat, trying to get a photograph of him. They would constantly telephone his flat, deluge him with letters, and even lie in wait for him at the hospital. As a shy person who is utterly dedicated to his professional calling, such attention became unbearable for Khan and he wanted absolutely nothing to do with it.

Local neighbours in Chelsea rallied around and tried their best to protect him. One elderly lady who lived in one of the flats below Khan once opened her window and poured water over the head of one Fleet Street journalist, just as they were trying to snap a picture of him.

It was an unusually negative response for somebody close to Diana. As far as other relationships had been concerned, the glamour of being with one of the most beautiful women in the world, who was dressed by the best designers, knew the world's leaders and attended all the best functions, tended to make the man next to her burst with male pride. Hasnat was just uncomfortable with the whole fame issue, and must have longed for her simply to be the 'girl next door'. It is a cliché, but actually it seems to ring true; for once somebody had fallen in love with her just for herself and not for all the trappings.

So while in the past her celebrity had been one of the main reasons that men wanted to know her, as far as Hasnat Khan was concerned it was the exact opposite. 'For the first time the public and the "power figure" didn't work in the way she wanted it to work, it was actually working against her,' says Devorik.

As a means of tackling Hasnat Khan's growing unease about the press, Diana started to plan more radical ways of escaping the limelight. She began to consider quite seriously the prospect of the two of them leaving Britain and living together in another country, as far from Fleet Street as could be engineered.

To this end she wrote to veteran heart surgeon Christian Barnard in South Africa, and she visited Australia's top heart clinic where Hasnat Khan had worked in the late eighties with Victor Chang, and she even scoured the United States for possible escape routes.

Her search for a foreign home where the two of them could live together and Hasnat could continue his work began on 13 October 1996. This was the day on which Diana flew to the northern Italian resort of Rimini where she was due to attend the annual congress of the Pio Manzù Centre, an international think tank led by former Soviet President Mikhail Gorbachev.

The assembly was attended by 350 academics, industrialists and health care experts, and its central theme was health. Diana was to be one of a number of people who would be honoured at the centre's annual awards ceremony, in recognition of her work in hospitals.

When she landed, the Princess was mobbed by cameramen and reporters, despite the combined best efforts of the Italian authorities. The streets had been sealed off, a helicopter hovered overhead, but even the army of Italian officials could not prevent the chaos that ensued in the foyer of the Grand Hotel.

On the opening day of the congress Diana delivered a speech on her chosen topic of 'The challenge of an ageing population'. Her main theme was that old age should not be seen as a disease. Sitting next to Diana that day was another award recipient, seventy-three-year-old Professor Christian Barnard.

The South African Professor had pioneered heart transplants in the late sixties and was using the Rimini platform to appeal for better prevention as well as treatment of the disease. Barnard told delegates about a young black boy he had operated on several years earlier, whose first words on waking were to ask for a piece of bread. Tearfully, he said the piece of bread came too late and the boy died clutching the piece of bread in his hand. Diana, clearly touched by the speech, leaned across and patted his shoulder as the Professor sat down.

In the evening the two of them sat next to each other at dinner, and Diana told the heart surgeon about Hasnat Khan. She asked Barnard if he could help Khan find a position in South Africa. It was an obvious choice of place to live; her brother Charles having already chosen to make Cape Town his home. Diana revealed to Barnard that she wanted to marry Khan and have a pair of girls. Barnard was to recall later that he was in no doubt that Diana was very much in love with Khan, and that she would have married him if he had agreed.[1]

1 *South African Sunday Times*, 22 November 1998

Diana had made it clear to the surgeon that she was serious about wanting to move away from London with Hasnat Khan, and on her return to London she telephoned, faxed and wrote to Barnard about job possibilities for him. Barnard was subsequently invited to dinner at Kensington Palace twice, to talk things over further with the Princess. Diana was a master at pre-planning everything, partly as a response to her insecurity and her need to feel in control of any given situation. The problem was she did not inform Hasnat Khan about the plans she was making for him with Barnard and this could only end in upset.

Almost casually Diana told Khan that Professor Barnard was in town and that he should meet him. The two men did in fact meet at London's Grosvenor House Hotel when Barnard asked Khan for his CV. Apparently under the impression that this was to do with job possibilities *after* he had finished his PhD, Khan duly sent it to him.

At the meeting Khan disclosed that he couldn't handle the publicity of living with Diana. Barnard told him that he himself had had to live with publicity ever since his first transplant operations. But he said there was a clear difference between the two of them. *His* publicity concerned his work whereas Hasnat's concerned the woman he loved, and he would just have to live with that![2]

After that meeting at the Grosvenor Hotel a job opportunity did come through at a hospital in America. Khan was told of the offer and, as Diana described to friends, 'went ballistic'. He wanted to finish his PhD under Professor Yacoub and was not even remotely interested in moving. The fact that Diana had been making plans behind his back had been exposed and he was furious.

One of the other places Diana had been exploring as somewhere they might live together was Sydney in Australia.

Hasnat had spent happy times there while training under Victor Chang in the late eighties and early nineties. On 31 October 1996 Diana left for Sydney on a four-day visit. Two

2 *South African Sunday Times*, 22 November 1998

Diana visiting the Royal Brompton Heart and Lung hospital in Chelsea.

Hasnat Khan leaving Northwick Park hospital carrying cardio equipment.

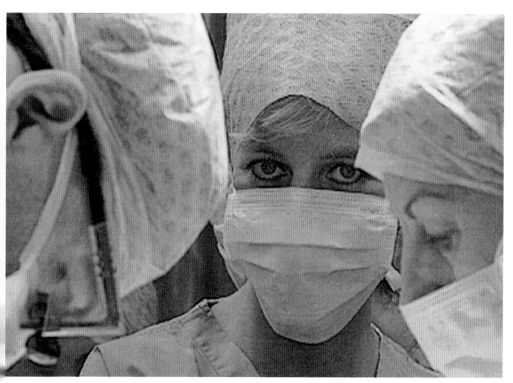

Attending a heart operation.

A treasured memory of a happy day.

Nanny Appa reflects sadly on the many cards and letters she and Diana exchange

'Anyone for tea'? Diana serves up the sandwiches at Kensington Palace for Hasnat Khan's family.

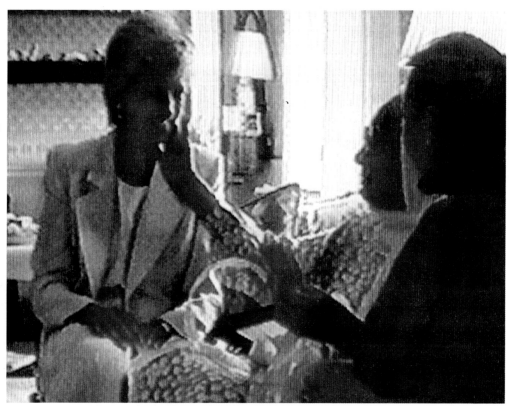

A moment of girlish delight as Nanny Appa opens her present of a silver bowl from Diana.

A younger Hasnat with his cousin Mumraiz.

Diana asked Appa for a photograph of herself and Hasnat, saying she would keep it with her always.

The Model Town house where Diana met Hasnat Khan's parents.

Daily life in Old Lahore.

Sunbathing with Dodi off the coast of Corsica. Diana senses she is being photographed but is not troubled.

The famous 'KISS' picture. Once thought to be a sneak photo, Diana had actually orchestrated it.

During the final cruise both Diana and Dodi were aware the photographs
were being taken.

Diana aboard the *Jonikal*, telephoning her confidants.

A stronger, more
confident woman
strides through the
minefields in Angola.

A devastated Hasnat
Khan at Diana's funeral.

Shedding the old image – Diana at London's Tate
gallery two months before her death.

years earlier, on 15 February 1994, the Victor Chang Institute had been established in memory of the murdered surgeon, and on 1 November 1996 Diana officially opened the Institute in its new premises in the Garvan Institute of Medical Research building in Victoria Street. Her visit raised 1 million Australian dollars for the cardiac centre.

Enthusiastic as she was to support the one good thing that had come out of Chang's untimely death, Diana hinted to friends that she had another purpose in visiting Sydney. She was using the trip to show Hasnat how her fame might be used for the causes close to his heart, and to install herself deeper into his life. While in Sydney she took the opportunity to meet an old medical friend of Hasnat's who was working at the Institute. She had missed the first three and a half decades of Hasnat Khan's life, but was catching up fast.

By now Diana's connections to all things medical were becoming too much of a coincidence for the press hounds of Fleet Street. Her visit to the little-known Victor Chang Institute began to raise suspicions about her real motives, and ultimately proved to be the final undoing of her secret.

And on 3 November 1996, the *Sunday Mirror* newspaper announced in bold headlines that they had made the connection between her midnight hospital visits, her attendance at heart operations and her current trip to Australia. It was all because she had fallen in love with Hasnat Khan.

The secret she had tried so hard to keep looked as if it was finally and inescapably out of the bag. Afraid this revelation would frighten Hasnat Khan away, Diana decided to take matters into her own hands, and turned to tried and trusted techniques to throw the press off the scent.

Richard Kay, the *Daily Mail*'s Court Correspondent, was a long-time trusted friend and ally of the Princess. Kay was with the press pack following her Sydney visit, and she turned to him with an article designed to counter the *Sunday Mirror*'s report. In it she rubbished the story of an affair with the doctor.

On the following day, 4 November, the *Daily Mail* article appeared, describing the *Sunday Mirror* report that she was in love with the doctor as 'bullshit'. The report stated that: 'She is understood to be deeply upset at the allegations because of the "hurt they do William and Harry". However she told friends: "It has given me a lot of laughs. In fact, we are laughing ourselves silly over this."

Diana scoffed at the claims that she wanted to marry the heart surgeon and have his babies, and Victoria Mendham was quoted as saying that the Princess thought the story was hysterical and it had caused them all great amusement, provoking much comment at breakfast.

But when Khan heard about the report, he was wounded and insulted. It almost brought their relationship to an immediate end, and at first he refused to see her. Diana protested that she had done it out of love for him and in order to protect him, but he said he thought it better they didn't see each other.

For three weeks not a word passed between them, although it wasn't for want of trying on Diana's part.

During those three weeks, according to Simmons, it was all she could do to prevent Diana from literally pounding the streets looking for him.

Eventually Hasnat Khan did get back in touch, but it appears there was an element of doubt after the Sydney incident, about how his life could be affected by the press, that lodged itself in Khan's brain and refused to go away.

Determined not to let the same mistake happen again, Diana tried a new tack. She set out to attempt to understand Hasnat Khan better through learning about their cultural differences. She had at least two copies of the Koran: one given to her by the Imam during her first visit to Pakistan in 1991 and another given to her by the houseboy at the Monnoo house in 1996. She took to reading the Koran every night. Lady Elsa Bowker says Diana would have converted to Islam, if she established that religion was a stumbling block with Hasnat's family that prevented her from marrying Khan.

To help bridge the communication gap between them she turned to Martin Bashir, the *Panorama* interviewer. Diana had stayed in touch with Bashir after the television programme and now she asked him to intervene in her troubled relationship with Hasnat. She told friends that she thought Bashir would be better able to interpret difficulties from an Asian point of view as opposed to her own European way. Also Bashir was some-body who she felt to be in her own court, a means therefore of maintaining a form of control.

So Bashir met Hasnat at Diana's request on several occasions. The two would spend evenings in the pub together. But things didn't quite go the way Diana had predicted. According to an account she gave a close friend the two men thoroughly enjoyed their get-togethers and at the end of the evening Diana would get a phone call from Hasnat saying he was going straight home to sleep. Diana didn't know whether this was true or not, but she was furious at the way things were turning out!

Realizing that this wasn't actually helping her own agenda, she turned instead to her trusted butler, Paul Burrell, saying she wanted to ask a special favour.

Burrell had never sat down in Diana's presence, as he did not feel it was his place to do so when he was working, and he didn't want to start now. Even when the Princess lit incense and a thick odorous fog drifted upwards to the ceiling he would crouch beneath it on his knees rather than take a seat to avoid the smoke.

One afternoon while tea was being served at Kensington Palace and Diana was seated on the floor with Simone Simmons, she started to broach the subject with Paul, who was dutifully standing next to her. She began delicately. Had he noticed sometimes when he arrived for work at seven in the morning that she looked as though she had not had any sleep and was still tired?

Burrell replied by saying that she always looked as fresh as a daisy. Diana persisted, saying, 'Have you noticed it or not? Tell me the truth.' The butler responded by saying it looked to him as though she had had a stressed rather than a relaxed sleep. Diana then launched into the topic at hand, saying, 'I'm going to tell you a secret, and you have to make a promise not to tell anyone.' Simmons says she told Burrell about her relationship with Hasnat Khan and so Burrell became a go-between. Both he and Bashir were sworn to secrecy.

Although Burrell's meetings with Khan still took place in a pub, he apparently preferred to stick to fizzy orange while acting on Diana's behalf. He and Khan soon became friends.

At times like this when Diana and Hasnat were not speaking, Diana's old insecurities would surface. Her behaviour became unsteady, irrational, uncontrolled. In an attempt to get through to Hasnat she would bombard the hospital switchboard with as many as twenty calls a day, using pseudonyms such as 'Dr Armani' and 'Dr Valentina', designer names lifted straight from the labels of her clothes. According to Simone Simmons, Diana tried every trick in the book to get hold of him. She rang the hospital using the cover of many different accents, drawing on her ability to impersonate. Sometimes she used a Liverpool accent copied from one of her favourite TV soaps, *Brookside*, sometimes she would adopt a phoney American accent. Once she even left a message claiming she was a sick patient and could Khan get back to her urgently.

Failing to reach Hasnat by phone she would try to engineer circumstances where she might see him, such as by arranging to go to the hospital to visit patients. But it didn't stop there. As with Oliver Hoare, her behaviour could take on the obsessive qualities of a stalker. In moods like this she proved herself capable of doing to others what she most hated being done to her.

She would watch Hasnat's front door for his comings and goings, while sitting in her car, desperate to glimpse even the slightest movement. Sometimes she would go for walks around

Knightsbridge in the middle of the night, unable to sleep, not knowing how to deal with the anxieties within her.

She was obsessing about Hasnat, as the perfect man for her, but on a more rational level, she did admit to herself that there were things about Hasnat that frustrated her, and some of this she would share with friends. She said that emotionally he appeared to be quite 'closed'. He didn't express how he felt towards her, and was 'quite undemonstrative'. For his part Khan, having had a stressful day in theatre, just wanted to put his feet up and relax. He admitted to a close relative that at times he found Diana too needy.

These responses, although quite natural to him, only served to increase her fear and paranoia. If Hasnat phoned his relatives in Pakistan from Kensington Palace, Diana would sometimes start thumping on the keys of the piano, or she might turn on some ballet music, turning the volume up higher and higher just to distract him, so that he would take notice of her.

During this three-week period of frustration and obsession, Diana once again called on the friendship of Simone Simmons. Simone lost count of the times that Diana would call her in a panic and ask her to go over to the Palace. 'She was in tears on the telephone, and I said, "Look, I'll come over and we'll talk about it." Diana said I couldn't come over, because she had been crying and she looked terrible, to which I replied, everyone looks terrible when they cry. Anyway after about forty-five minutes of talking on the telephone, Diana relented and said OK come over. So I went over and saw that Diana had great big panda eyes, and her nose was red. And we sat and talked about the problems in the relationship. Diana made cucumber and carrot juice, and I had a cup of tea. Diana was worried that she wasn't hearing from Hasnat. I said, "Look he's got his work to do, he's a heart surgeon, when he's doing a transplant there's no way he can drop everything and speak to you." She tried to understand that he was a busy man, and that when he was not working he was studying.'

In her relationship with Khan she was exhibiting many of the behavioural traits evident in her other relationships. She was incessantly phoning him the minute she believed he wasn't paying her any attention. She was seeking to involve herself as far as possible in his career by attending heart operations. She was doing her homework and trying to adapt to his life, by reading the Koran and wearing Pakistani clothes; after displaying her liking for the shalwar kameez she had several such outfits made for her own wardrobe. As with the other relationships she was using go-betweens who she hoped she could control when things threatened not to happen the way she wanted them to.

However, there were some positive changes to Diana's behaviour during this period. The lacerations she had inflicted on herself in times of great emotional stress in the past were no longer to be seen, and many of her friends noticed that she was gradually turning into a stronger person, a more confident individual.

Perhaps the key difference was that for once she was beginning to be able to differentiate between her personal and professional life. Having gained emotional and mental confidence, she was able to channel her energies into her work with an independent mind that was unassailed by her personal problems, and finally achieve something for herself.

Diana's greatest legacy, the landmines campaign, was to be proof of her newfound strength. It was to be another watershed.

17

'I wouldn't be seen dead in virtually any of them!'

'You see that little star over there, guess what it is', said Simone Simmons to Diana. 'I don't know,' replied the Princess. 'That's a landmine,' announced Simmons. During the summer of 1996 the energy healer had spent ten days in Bosnia, staying with a Red Cross worker in Tuzla. When she returned, she took her photographs of the visit to Kensington Palace to show Diana.

The photos graphically illustrated the post-civil war way of life in Bosnia. One picture showed two children hand in hand walking around what clearly still resembled a war zone, and there was a photograph of a landmine that had been planted in the road. 'People haven't got enough food there. They can't just walk into a shop, because there aren't any,' Simmons told the Princess. 'How do people eat then?' asked Diana. 'They rely on the things they can catch with their own hands: rabbits, chickens, fish or whatever.'

The way people were clearly still suffering, as captured in her friend's Bosnia pictures, grabbed Diana's attention. She looked at Simmons with a serious expression on her face and said, 'Do you think I could make a difference?' Simmons replied, 'Well, if you can't, then nobody can!' It was the start of a process that was to bring her face to face with her greatest challenge so far, and, many would say, ultimately her greatest single achievement.

Diana hadn't been hearing about landmines only from Simone. Mike Whitlam, the then Director General of the Red Cross, had sent a package of literature and videos about landmines to Kensington Palace. He had been looking for a way to bring the campaign into the headlines after its initial launch. It was Whitlam who also asked filmmaker Richard Attenborough to invite the Princess to be guest of honour at the première of his new film, *In Love and War*, which was destined to raise money for the British Red Cross landmines appeal.

As she leafed through Whitlam's brochures, Diana read that the most densely concentrated area for landmines was in Cambodia and, fired by a sense of outrage and the sense of a mission to be fulfilled, Diana decided she wanted to go there. But it was more difficult to arrange than she had at first appreciated, and eventually she was prevented from making the journey because the Foreign Office said her presence in Cambodia could upset delicate negotiations they were holding over a British hostage who was in the hands of rebel forces there. So Diana switched her focus to Angola instead, where the grim statistics suggested that there was one landmine for every one of its twelve million inhabitants.

Diana announced her trip to Angola under the auspices of the Red Cross. It was the beginning of what was to become a successful public campaign for Diana, one that would provide her with the clearest focus in her public life since she left the Royal Family.

The four-day trip was planned for the middle of January and before Diana left she discussed her packing arrangements for Angola with Simmons. Simone advised her that if she wanted to make an impact then she should dress down, because what she was highlighting wasn't herself but what the victims of landmines were going through. On this advice Diana left her designer clothes in the wardrobe, and never wore dresses or skirts, but jeans and shirts instead. Only once did she bend the rules when she wore an old dress to the Governor's dinner.

The victims of the landmines deeply affected Diana; she was genuinely upset by what she saw and according to Simone she was in tears every night. Diana telephoned her friend at least once a day without fail. The conversations would start with 'Angola calling Hendon; come in, Hendon!'

Diana talked each day about the sights she had seen and how much they had disturbed her. She described how on 14 January she met thirteen-year-old Sandra Tigica during a visit to a hospital. Sandra had been walking home to her parents' farm when a plane dropped a bomb which tore off one of her legs. She had been waiting for an artificial limb ever since. Throughout their ten-minute chat, during which Sandra's stump was being measured up for an artificial limb, Diana tenderly stroked the frightened young girl's arm and later cuddled her. She told Simone that to stop herself crying she had to bite the side of her mouth.

She also spoke of her infamous walk through an Angolan minefield on 15 January. Diana's visit had generated huge controversy back home in London, particularly because of her statement that she was 'pleased to assist the Red Cross in its campaign to ban once and for all, antipersonnel landmines'. The sentiment ran counter to British government policy at the time. Television and radio news were full of the story, as were the newspapers, and Diana was being described as a 'loose cannon'. It only served to make the Princess more determined, and she hit back with a big media message. She offered a dramatic photo opportunity, not subversively as she had done in the past, but up front, full camera.

She decided to walk through the minefield, in front of the world's cameras, while protesting that she was a humanitarian figure and she was only trying to help. What the world didn't see was her fear. Although she was wearing a face protector and flak jacket, she later told Simmons the walk had terrified her.

The landmines campaign was a catalyst for Diana to get out there and do something to make a difference. The *Daily Telegraph* columnist Lord Deedes called the Angola trip a watershed, though in truth it was probably just the first public sign of a private watershed she had reached some time earlier.

The visit represented a true initiative on Diana's part, and besides her appearance being much more casual – she was no longer the 'dressed-up Royal' – the campaign represented the pinnacle of what Diana had achieved within herself. It was a measure of her own internal growth.

The realization that she could influence political agendas gave Diana an enormous release, a burst of freedom. She felt she was really discovering her true vocation and her mission in life, and that she had found a means of promoting her self-esteem and boosting her confidence which did not rely on another person. Diana felt more powerful, she could see she had the means to get things moving, and she had the where-withal to force something that in her view was 'right' into the line of public awareness.

Although she was in love with Hasnat Khan during this period, she was actually a lot more secure in herself as a human being; so the emotional insecurities were not dictating how things turned out on the professional front, and her personal growth was no longer dependent on whether she was being loved or not.

She was happier with life in general and as a result of this she was becoming more open, more self-accepting and was blaming other people far less often. Most importantly she increasingly began to like herself, which in turn meant she could *conceive* of reaching a situation where she actually had the right amount of love in her life.

Furnished with this new inner confidence, and the burgeon-ing feeling that at last she was loved for herself, Diana had the strength to reshape her public life and take control. She was making her own plans, devising her own itineraries and proving just how much she could do on her own.

It seemed at least to be the *start* of her release from self-doubt and insecurity. The emotional limpet seemed to be disappear-ing.

The fact she appeared to be getting mentally stronger was also reflected in her body shape. As she gained control over her body, her daily work outs at the gym resulted in Diana becoming bigger, and her shape assumed healthy womanly proportions. Gone were the self-inflicted scratches and lacerations. The nervous giggles were being replaced by throaty laughs.

The sense that she was developing a belief in her self-worth and purpose is also marked by a change in her clothes. At home Diana scuttled about happily in bare feet, while in public she was poised in high heels. By 1994 she had firmly established her own identity in her clothes; at that time they were slinky and colourful. Before then she had never gone for primary colours. After 1995 her clothes were close fitting, there were no more petticoats or bustles. When such distinct shifts in her dress style are noted, it is not surprising that another of the side effects of her landmines campaign was one that affected her wardrobe. But this wasn't another relatively superficial design statement; it was about as big a sartorial signpost as you can imagine.

It was Diana's announcement that she was planning a sale of her most famous dresses.

In her terms it was a truly powerful statement that really said that she was putting her Royal life well and truly behind her, and from now on, *she* was in the driving seat.

The idea was really that of her son William – perhaps there is more than just a facial resemblance between mother and son. When Diana was in Barbuda during Christmas 1996 William phoned her and announced, 'I've had a brilliant idea, Mum, why don't you have a sale of your dresses for charity – and I'll take ten per cent!'

Diana thought about it while relaxing on the beach, and decided it really *was* a brilliant idea. When she arrived back from Barbuda she phoned Simone Simmons, told her about the plan and invited her friend over to help her go through all the wardrobes and root out the main contenders for the auction.

Diana kept her evening gowns in a room below the main

apartment. Upstairs, on a level with the 'little lounge', was her dressing room. This was a totally new snapshot of Diana. Simmons describes how she walked into the room housing Diana's ball gowns and it was like an Aladdin's cave. She just couldn't resist touching the dazzling outfits; they were out of this world. Certainly there was nothing like it in any shop in Hendon!

Together, the two women waded through the near priceless collection. Diana said the first things she wanted to get rid of were what she called the 'dowdy frumpy outfits'. 'I actually don't need these any more,' she said. Despite their obvious splendour, Simmons had to agree. 'No, you're not going to need them.'

It was a strange feeling for Simone; trying to sound as if she was giving good advice, when faced with a wardrobe which other women would kill for! But she reminded herself that Diana respected Simone's objectivity, and so she said, 'Forget the sentimentality, which of these things would you wear again?' Diana looked around, and then around again and pointed to one dress, 'I could wear *that*!', at which Simone laughed and said, 'Yes, in Queen Elizabeth I's time maybe!' Diana burst out laughing, and then seemed to realize that she didn't really need *any* of them. 'I wouldn't be seen dead in virtually any of them!' she said. 'Right, all of those are going!'

It took Diana and Simone an afternoon and the best part of an evening to clear out the dresses.

In late January she announced that she would be holding a sale of her dresses that June. It was certainly an original way to make money, and Diana announced that the proceeds would be divided between AIDS Crisis Trust and the Cancer Research Fund for the Royal Marsden Hospital.

The dress sale was not the only sign of major change at this time. Diana began to reduce her dependency on healers and therapists, for so long her mainstay, and one which had become such a major part in her everyday life that it must almost have been like a blind man throwing away his cane. Simmons believes she would eventually have kicked her most enduring therapeutic habit, that of colonic irrigation, because now Diana was getting her 'treatment from life'.

Simmons herself can be described as an 'alternative' therapist, given that she provides something which is not available through – or even endorsed by – the National Health Service. But even she was amazed by the next insight she was given into Diana's old, cluttered life.

In the downstairs room where Diana kept her ball gowns, the Princess pointed out a cupboard on the wall. Simone says, 'Diana opened it up; it was overflowing with complementary medicines of every imaginable kind. Vitamins, minerals, liver extract; you name it, everything was there. I said, "My God what's all this for?" I looked at one of the containers and said, "It's out of date", and Diana said, "Stay where you are, I'll be back in a tick." A few minutes later she returned with a great big, black bin bag that she'd found somewhere.'

Over the years countless therapists had given the Princess different 'cures'; remedies to pep her up, pills to calm her down. Simmons says to imagine walking into a health shop, and see all the potions on offer, and that's what Diana had, all in that one cupboard. But now it was throwaway time – almost everything was destined for the bin bag. Together, the two women went through everything, separating things which Diana might need in an emergency from the things that she would never need at all or were completely useless.

It was another massive clearout. After it was all over, Diana said, 'God, it looks empty!' In the waste sack they reckoned they had probably dumped thousands of pounds' worth of treatments – all discarded as part of Diana's much wider cure.

The press, meanwhile, continued their attempts to expose her relationship with Hasnat. Fully aware of Khan's aversion to the press and afraid that the relentless pursuit of them both could damage their relationship, Diana was going to enormous extremes to put them off the trail.

There were the disguises: the long black and brown wigs and

glasses, the circuitous routes around town to make sure no one was following her, and the manufacture of false stories with the aid of one or two trusted Fleet Street journalists.

On top of these methods, she also recruited the help of friends in protecting Hasnat Khan from the press.

This was not a new tactic; she had often used friends in putting the press off the scent. In fact she did it to such an extent that a former press secretary admitted it was sometimes difficult to do the job not always knowing what Diana had told one of her friends to say.

In January 1997 Clive Goodman, the Royal reporter for the *News of the World,* was on the trail again but this time was planning to write an exposé of her relationship with Hasnat Khan. On hearing this, Diana asked Simone Simmons to call the reporter and say that the Princess was still seeing Oliver Hoare. Simone was to add that if he didn't believe her, Goodman could catch the Princess walking up and down outside Hoare's house that evening. Diana told Simmons that as a back-up, she would also ring her personal assistant Victoria Mendham and instruct her to confirm the story about Hoare, oblivious, it seems, to any potential upset this may or may not have caused the art dealer.

Mendham, then twenty-seven years old, had been working for Diana for seven years and had become a close personal friend. But when Diana tried to get hold of Mendham she was out. Goodman, however, succeeded where Diana had failed, and managed to track down Victoria Mendham who, blissfully ignorant of Diana's ploy, naturally denied that the relationship with Hoare was still current.

Diana was furious at this and Mendham was given her marching orders on 23 January after seven years at the Palace. Newspaper reports at the time said the sacking was purportedly over a money dispute following the Christmas holiday in the Caribbean island of Barbuda. It appears more likely that Diana had come to expect a level of complicity from those around her and in this case could not accept it when Mendham went against Diana's cover story.

Throughout this time, Diana had been maintaining her contacts with Hasnat Khan's family. Her newfound confidence hadn't dampened her wish to be a part of his family. In January 1997, Omar and Jane, Hasnat's aunt and uncle in Stratford-upon-Avon, had their first baby. Diana had been involved with the whole pregnancy and was almost as excited about the arrival of a newborn baby as were the parents. The baby was named Dyan, after the Princess.

Diana had been doing the rounds of the maternity shops, as if it were her own baby, and she had bought a pram, a pushchair and all sorts of baby clothes. Now she arrived again at their house having driven herself up from London.

During her stay at Stratford, she helped to put the new baby's pram together. Professor Jawad Khan had also arrived; he had just flown in from Pakistan to see his new nephew. He remembers the two of them, a heart surgeon and a Princess, assembling a pram! Neither of them had ever done such a thing before. Diana was joking to Omar and Jane that it was like an Italian Ferrari, and she was telling them how to drive it.

Diana certainly felt very involved with the new arrival. On another occasion she turned up at Omar and Jane's house and announced, 'You go out now. Take as long as you like. I am babysitting.'

Diana was developing a strong friendship with Jane and invited her to stay at Kensington Palace. Jane seemed to be able to help bring Diana back down to earth, and obviously continued to pass on her experience of having married into the Pathan clan. Diana learned from Jane that acceptance had taken a lot of persuasion and a lot of patience, and Diana knew that if she wanted to marry Hasnat, she had to go down the same route.

The person she needed to persuade above all was Hasnat's mother, and she knew that was not going to be an easy task.

18

Caught between a rock and a hard place

The town of Jhelum in northern Pakistan lies one hundred and ninety-five kilometres north of the city of Lahore, on the 'GT' road, or grand trunk road. Members of the Khan family regularly travel between the two, visiting the respective family homes in Model Town and the former glass factory on the outskirts of Jhelum. The roads are bumpy and ill maintained in the extreme, judging by the volcano-like craters where roads have simply caved in. Pedestrians have a nasty habit of running out into the road, rather than simply insinuating themselves into the traffic as they might in New York or London. Perhaps it is as good a means to cross as any other; but not surprisingly many are killed. On top of it all, you can hardly see anything; vision is almost totally impaired by the clouds of dust that are whirled up like mini tornadoes from the unpaved streets on either side of the main roads.

About five kilometres to the north of Jhelum, on the left-hand side, the main road slopes away and you can spot an old sign reading 'Prime Glass'. This is the estate of the Khan family that once rang out to the manufacture of the country's glassware. Now, however, the old factory building is silent, and what used to be its administrative block has been turned into a junior and upper school run by one of Hasnat Khan's sisters.

Thick, ochre-coloured walls form the circumference of what was once a privileged and wealthy establishment, now tinged with faded grandeur.

Further into the estate the road swings round and gives way to an imposing house with a wide sweeping veranda. This is the so-called 'Little House' in which Hasnat Khan grew up. Somehow it seems reminiscent of the old plantation houses found in America's deep south.

The buff-painted sitting room, like so many of these old houses, has vast cavernous ceilings. It is winter so the ceiling fans are silent; the huge fireplace in the centre of the room no doubt crackles with the sound of burning firewood in the late evenings, but it is mid-morning and so the house is still. The décor is plain and simple, reflecting a life lived without fuss. The red-tiled floor is lined with rugs, and there are leather stools dotted around the room.

Outside, on the veranda, there is suddenly movement and a medium-built figure dressed in a maroon velour shalwar kameez appears. It is Hasnat's mother. Described even by members of her own family as formidable and very headstrong, there is a degree of apprehension in this encounter.

An aunt, one of many, who is on a weekend visit to see her sister's family, appears and busies herself making sure everyone is seated while she organizes tea. There's no gas in Jhelum, so the process of cooking lunch or any other meal has to be carefully planned, and must of necessity start around three hours before it's needed. Even light refreshments are an extraordinary feat of achievement.

Naheed Khan was born in 1931, the eldest child of Appa. She has a Master of Arts degree and in the early fifties when she was studying, such a woman would have been regarded as extremely liberal and broad minded.

As she begins to speak it is clear she is an articulate individual who has arrived at her opinions after much careful reflection. She is direct, and speaks straight from the heart, which is unusual amongst the elders of this Muslim society.

153

Her once fine features have hardened with time, but there is no loss of ardour and passion in her voice as she now spells out her views to another member of the clan. An insight into the mother's thinking brings with it an understanding of the nature of the difficulty there might have been concerning marriage plans between Hasnat Khan and Diana.

Naheed Khan begins by expressing her resentment towards the British Raj on the subcontinent. She doesn't like the influence the British had on Pakistan, and the upheaval caused to everyone's lives. At the time of partition in 1947, Naheed Khan was sixteen. She witnessed one of the biggest population transfers in history when the boundary was defined between the thoroughly mixed Muslim–Hindu areas of the Punjab and Bengal. When the so-called Radcliffe Line was announced, Muslims fled one way across it and Hindus and Sikhs the other; in all some six million souls in each direction.

In riots and terrible massacres on both sides somewhere between two hundred thousand and a million people were killed. It was at about this time that Naheed Khan and her parents left their home town of Ferozepur in what is now India before moving to Lahore, which is only a matter of miles from the border. The memories of those times are still fresh and sharp in Naheed Khan's mind.

About 10 per cent of Pakistani society belongs to the upper class or elite. These people are highly educated and exposed to Western influences. That means they do not follow the joint family systems as closely as the lower and middle class. Faced with a society that is changing rapidly, and having to adapt to the modern ways of materialism and commercialism, Naheed Khan makes it clear that she fundamentally dislikes the influence the West is having on her society, and more importantly on the culture. But while her family has been influenced by the West, the younger generation are still bound by traditional values and respect for their elders. It creates a conflict which someone in Hasnat's position finds himself in the middle of.

In India there are castes, in Pakistan there are clans, which form the moral backbone and social bedrock with which that society structures the way it lives. Hasnat Khan and his family belong to a clan called the Pathans. The Pathans are descendants of a very proud, conservative race of warriors that live primarily in Afghanistan and Pakistan. Although their origin is unclear, their legends suggest that they are descendants of Afghana, grandson of King Saul. However, most scholars believe that they probably arose from ancient Aryans intermingling with subsequent invaders.

Lying right at the core of the Pathan society is the notion of the extended family, and compared to all other ethnic groups in Pakistan, the family structure of the Pathans is one of the strongest and most close knit.

Naheed Khan is committed to the belief that the joint family system is the one that works best in this culture and society. She is a traditionalist who endorses a system whereby the mother and father bring up the children, then their children look after the parents, with three generations living under the same roof. To her, this is the way that a society can keep itself together.

The joint system was in operation within the Khan family as she spoke. An aunt returned to the veranda carrying a child, the first son of Hasnat's younger brother, Memuhn. The boy's parents were absent, but still someone in the family was there to care for him. In turn that baby will become the 'favourite' nephew of someone else from within the family, and the child will then receive special love, not just from its parents, but from another close family member as well.

This is how the joint family system works. The family is a cushion; it provides security, and if someone suffers the modern-day affliction of unemployment, for instance, then the family will look after that person. The family is the key to survival, but it can also impose a huge, inescapable onus of responsibility on any one member of the family, as a balance to providing a security net. It works fine as long as everyone shares all the ambitions and ideals of the clan.

This is the system Hasnat Khan, an intelligent man with ambitions to perfect his skills as a heart surgeon, grew up in.

Hasnat was adopted by his uncle Jawad, who treated him as if he were his own son; helping him with his career and finding job opportunities for him. In turn, Hasnat adopted Jawad's eldest son Mumraiz as his own. Within such a system most marriages are arranged. Families will know each other and various relatives will be married to each other. In such marriages, the parents are like counsellors; if a couple is having a problem it will be sorted out by the family. Marriage is not just about two people, but is seen as an opportunity for the whole family to come together. It is a division of life and work.

Hasnat's parents had already tried to marry their eldest son off twice before in 1987 and 1992. But in each case he procrastinated and the wedding never took place. A third engagement, this time of his own choosing, also failed to result in marriage.

Although Hasnat Khan has spent a considerable proportion of his life in the West, and is used to a different system, this is the culture he has grown up with. Even though he probably does not want an arranged marriage, for him to take unilateral decisions about his relationships would be like breaking the ground rules and dividing the family.

When a marriage is to take place there are other considerations that are made in this society – the reputation of the person is very important, as is the reputation of that person's family. As a son, it is usual to share the parents' house, and vice versa, so can the girl get along with your parents? Will she be able to live in the same house as your parents? This is a big problem if a girl has grown up in the West – how is she going to come and live in a joint family system?

Although liberal and forward thinking now, historically the Pathans were reluctant to accept anyone from outside their own clan. They have a lot of pride in who they are, even though the Punjab is not originally their area, and they stick to their old traditions. Even marrying another Asian from a different group tends to be thought of as a mixed marriage.

Such a marriage to an 'outsider' has happened in the Khan family, in the case of Omar and Jane. Omar is Professor Jawad's younger brother. He was brought up in England and had got used to the ways of the West. When he first approached the family about marrying Jane, a British girl, there was a lot of opposition to the proposed match. In particular, Appa's husband, Professor Ayub Ahmad Khan, also a doctor, was totally against it, insisting on the importance of a sense of belonging. He believed that in a mixed marriage this sense of belonging would be diluted.

Omar and Jane had known each other for several years. The family realized Omar was not going to marry anyone else, so it fell to Appa and her eldest son Jawad to decide what the family should do. In the end, two years after the father had died, Jane and Omar got married. Their wedding took place on the lawn at the house in Model Town.

The power of the mother figure cannot be underestimated in this society, and as Professor Akbar Ahmed had illustrated for Diana, Islam has a lot of respect for the mother. In fact it's not just respect but something that goes much deeper. Hasnat's uncle Ashfaq elaborates that, 'Eastern boys are very much in love with their mothers. This is not a Freudian theory, but this is a reality, and they think and believe (and the Koran says) that paradise lies at the feet of the mother. There is a famous saying in our religion that if you irritate your mother you will be tortured in this life and hereafter.' According to Ashfaq the maternal influence crosses continents and cultures. Hasnat 'cannot budge an inch from the dictates of his mother, even if he has spent so much time in England and he has lived in that society and he has seen liberty and freedom from close quarters; he wouldn't say no to his mother in any affair.'

The relationship between mother and son is very close, and she would have an influence on every aspect of his life. Jawad Khan will drop everything for Appa even now, even though he is an important surgeon, in his fifties, and has four of his own children. The call of the mother is so strong that it will come before that of his wife and family.

It is not uncommon for sons to divorce their wives because of their mother's influence. In one case, a couple had been quite happily married for four years, but the mother didn't like certain of her daughter-in-law's habits. The couple occasionally argued, as everyone does, but the parents would be listening. The mother would think 'how dare my daughter-in-law argue with my son'. In the end the mother broke up the marriage, even though her son loved his wife and wanted to stay with her.

Mothers like their sons to live with them; in the Khan family there is pressure on Hasnat's younger brother, Memuhn, to live with his parents, as Hasnat is not there. Naheed misses Hasnat being at home, and in turn he feels a sense of responsibility, because he knows he should be there for his parents.

The longer Hasnat lives in the West, the harder it becomes for him to make a commitment to marry a Pakistani woman, and so the deeper his dilemma grows. As he gets older the pressure to marry increases. His other brothers and sisters are all married now, and Naheed's aim in life is to see Hasnat married to someone from within the Pathan clan. He feels obliged; he feels it is his duty; he feels he would be letting his parents down; it would be a betrayal and he would ostracize himself if he went against his parents' wishes. Yet at the same time he is now thoroughly Westernized; he finds it difficult to entertain the idea of an arranged marriage, having got used to the ways of the West. When he goes back to Pakistan he is only there for two weeks at the most, which is definitely not long enough to get to know someone.

So Hasnat is caught between a rock and a hard place – unable to make a decision, unable to commit himself.

All of this was in Khan's mind in the spring of 1997. Those close to the family say Hasnat was definitely in love with Diana and he wanted to marry her. His uncle Ashfaq says, 'If you probe deep into the emotions and the dormant feelings of Hasnat, I can say with certainty that he was greatly in love with that lady, and he was very much impressed by her personality, not by her beauty, but by her humanity.'

Being aware of his family ties, and of the problems that his culture would impose, Hasnat reportedly said to Diana that she should go over and see Pakistan for herself, go and see Lahore, go and see Islamabad, go and see his house and his lifestyle.

To him, the fact that Diana was an icon, an international celebrity, conflicted with his own lifestyle and his own tightly knit family. He could not see how Diana could adjust to that, and he told her so. Diana, desperate to prove Hasnat wrong, and anxious to save the relationship by showing Hasnat it could work, agreed to go to Pakistan to see Hasnat's mother and father, and his close family. She felt sure if the family met her they would like her, and that she could win them round, and Hasnat would then find it easier to commit himself.

In the course of a telephone conversation with his parents in Pakistan, Khan asked his mother if she would meet Diana. Events were to move one stage further . . .

Part Four
The Final Summer

19

'I want to marry Hasnat Khan'

Diana set off for Lahore for the third time on 22 May 1997 for a three-day visit, flying there on a private Boeing 757 belonging to Sir James Goldsmith. She was travelling with Goldsmith's daughter, Jemima Khan, and Jemima's six-month-old son Sulaiman. Her spirits were high as, only the night before, Britain's new prime minister, Tony Blair, had imposed a total ban on the sale of landmines. When Diana heard the news she jumped up, punched a fist into the air and yelled, 'Yesss!'[1]

On this visit to Pakistan Diana was staying with Imran Khan at his house in the Zaman Park neighbourhood of the city. The house is a red-brick seventies compound shared between Imran and Jemima, the elder Mr Khan, and the family of one of his daughters. The arched front door opens into a spartan white-washed hallway, and polished stone steps lead up to Imran and Jemima's self-contained apartment.

Diana's room was adjacent to Imran and Jemima's one-bed flat. The walls were hung with rich Eastern tapestries, and her bed nestled into a cosy alcove.

As far as the outside world was concerned Diana was in Lahore in order to pay another charity visit to Imran's cancer hospital. She was due to launch a new endowment fund appeal to help towards keeping the hospital open. However, she was

1 *Sunday Mirror*, 9 November 1997

killing two birds with one stone. Passionate as she was about Imran's hospital, this event provided a convenient cover for the main event.

Her personal quest and the main reason for being in Lahore was to visit Hasnat's family; to try to persuade his mother that she was a suitable match for her eldest son.

Imran and Jemima had invited a dozen couples over to their house to meet the Princess shortly after her arrival. The dinner was being held in the back garden of the Khan house, surrounded by tall bamboo trees, and lit by fairy lights hanging from the branches. A marquee had been erected from which the food would be served. Diana stood at the head of the queue with Imran and Jemima, greeting guests as they arrived.

One of those invited was Jugnu Mohsin, an irreverent journalist and sharp critic of people in power, who she regularly vilified for their abuses of the system. Now at the helm of the Lahore-based *Friday Times* newspaper, she had previously spent seven years in England, studying law at Cambridge.

At dinner Mohsin sat next to Diana and the two women were soon chatting. Diana began to show real interest when Mohsin told her she considered herself to be a very modern Pakistani woman, a composite personality who had spent her formative years in England but then returned to her native Pakistan.

Mohsin said that Diana was greatly interested in the concept of a woman being 'of the modern world' on the one hand, but also thriving in a traditional conservative Muslim country like Pakistan.

'The idea of being able to marry the two cultures and to live productively and creatively in that sort of milieu appealed enormously to the Princess.'

She asked Mohsin if her marriage had been 'arranged'. Mohsin answered that she was 'lucky'; she met her husband and got to know him before they were married, and that he had given her all his support. 'So he's a modern man?' said Diana, 'Yes, absolutely,' replied the journalist.

They continued talking about what life was like in Pakistan;

what the main difficulties were, what the benefits were, the security the family provided, and Mohsin felt that the recurring theme of unconditional love and support that Eastern families provide was a powerful lure for Diana.

During the dinner Diana decided she wanted to move indoors, and invited Mohsin to accompany her. The journalist followed Diana into Imran's house where the politician's nephews were playing cricket in the living room. Diana turned to Mohsin and said, 'I really feel at home here.'

It is not difficult to piece together some of the thoughts that were going through Diana's mind that evening. She was weighing up the prospects of being able to inhabit two worlds at once, and she was feeling comfortable with the idea. It fired her with renewed determination to win Hasnat's family over.

By now, the time had come to meet Hasnat Khan's parents. But first of all a location for the meeting had to be agreed. Imran wanted it to be at his house, for her ease and convenience, but Hasnat's family felt that if Diana had come all this way to meet them then they should play host to her at their home in Model Town. In the end the matter was resolved after Hasnat's mother rang Diana. Between them they discussed the pros and cons of the choices and eventually agreed that Diana would go to Model Town at around five o'clock that afternoon.

Diana got ready, changing into a blue shalwar kameez that Jemima had had made for her in Lahore. Although a little apprehensive, she appeared quite excited and seemed to be looking forward to meeting new members of the family, meeting up with Appa again, and of course being able to chat with Hasnat's parents. Although she was prepared for the mother Naheed being 'headstrong', Hasnat's father Rasheed was described as being gentle, a quiet man who had spent his life creating fine hand-blown pieces of glass.

It was agreed that two of Imran Khan's sisters, Aleema and Rhanee, would accompany the Princess. Rhanee knew Hasnat Kahn's family well, and thirty-nine-year-old Aleema had met the Princess before during her 1996 trip to Pakistan, and had discussed the design of her dresses with Rizwan Beyg and Jemima. Like Diana, Aleema had two sons, aged fifteen and twelve.

The one thing the party wanted to avoid at all costs was press attention, so it was decided that Aleema would drive Diana there in her own black Toyota Corolla, so as not to raise undue suspicion. Whenever Diana made a trip anywhere she was normally accompanied by a cavalcade of police security vehicles, but on this occasion the three women gave the security men the slip, and travelled to Model Town unescorted, but undetected.

The fact that Diana had flown to Pakistan to meet the Khan family was proof of her serious intentions, and she believed she had a real chance to persuade Hasnat's family that she could be good enough for her son. Somewhere in Hasnat's mind there must also have been some hope of this for him to speak to his mother about meeting Diana in the first place.

Meanwhile eleven close members of Hasnat's family – his brother and sisters and their husbands, his Aunt Maryam and her husband Salahuddin, Appa, Uzma, Professor Jawad's wife, and of course Hasnat's mother and father – were gathering at the Model Town home. Hasnat's parents had travelled the one hundred and ninety-five kilometres from their own house in Jhelum especially for the meeting.

It was late afternoon and the light was beginning to fade. Day was rapidly turning to dusk. The soft scent of jasmine wafted through the air and mosquitoes began to comb the air in preparation for their night raids. It was a hundred degrees Fahrenheit, and the heat was sauna-like and ennervating.

Slowly Diana's black Toyota pulled into the sweeping driveway in front of the house. Diana emerged onto the cool porch and shook hands with the family members, and with Hasnat's mother and father. It was to be the first and only time the two women would meet.

Power cuts are not uncommon in Pakistan; they are a regular feature of life in a country whose infrastructure has been steadily eroded by successive governments running further and further into debt. But now, as the lights went out just as Diana was arriving in Model Town this common occurrence somehow took on sinister overtones.

For now, though, having no light was just a minor inconvenience, and wooden chairs were simply arranged on the lawns of the house under the mango and palms trees. Inside the house Aunt Maryam was busy organizing tea. Groping around in the darkness of a kitchen cupboard she managed to find some Staffordshire stoneware cups with a flower motif. Only five cups and saucers matched, the rest would have to be assembled from the oddments collected and handed down over the years.

The tea, along with some patties and pastries bought hastily from a nearby shop, were put onto an old wooden trolley with rickety wheels and navigated by the servants down the porch steps and into the garden.

The family was talking about the lights going out and, laughing, Diana said there was also a water shortage at Imran's house. She seemed to accept that such things go hand in hand with life in Pakistan and did not seem particularly bothered by them.

Everyone had hand fans to keep cool in the heat.

The atmosphere was one of friendly informality. Salahuddin, Aunt Maryam's husband, commented on Diana's dress, asking her where she had got it. She told him that it was from Jemima, and made in Lahore. He joked that *his* shalwar was made by Rifat Ozbek (a celebrated Turkish designer).

The word had been spreading around the neighbourhood that Princess Diana was here, and a substantial group of nosy neighbours was peering through the gates and into the garden. Salahuddin had to go and rebuke them, asking them to allow his family some peace, as this gathering was to discuss a private matter.

Salahuddin went to fetch his camera, and used an entire roll of film to mark the event. Everything was very amicable; it seemed to be going well.

Amidst all the conviviality lurked the need to win over Naheed Khan. Diana took tea, but didn't eat anything, which suggested she was more nervous and anxious about this than she seemed on the surface. The two women talked together. It was just informal chitchat, not by any means a close or intimate conversation.

Hasnat's parents asked nothing that would suggest they viewed Diana seriously as a potential match for their son, and she in return said nothing in words to try to convince them that she should be their daughter-in-law. It was simply a chance to eye each other up, to get a feel for the kind of person each was.

The lights suddenly came back on, and the party moved indoors. In a small room adjoining the main lounge the children had thrown themselves down on scattered cushions and were watching television. Diana joined them and together they watched cartoons: *Penelope Pitstop* and *Wacky Races*. An hour or so later, Diana left.

After the meeting with the family Diana went straight back to Imran Khan's house. Her mood was much more sombre and contemplative than it had been before.

On the way back she talked with Aleema Khan, mulling over her future and what she should do. She told Aleema about how the press upset her, how she didn't like the fact that journalists sold stories about her for their own financial gain. She felt betrayed by the people who sold articles and were willing to talk about her relationships.

She also told Aleema that she would like to live in Australia, feeling that the press would leave her alone more there, or at least it would be less intense.

She said that Hasnat Khan was the only person who had not talked about her to anyone else. He hadn't sold his story to the press, it was the sort of thing he could probably never do, and she said she respected that.

Aleema told the Princess about how she would like to have a

couple of daughters in the future, and Diana said she would like to have one as well. She told Aleema that she was pleased she had met the family. But she also said she was keen to pursue her landmines campaign, and the fundraising efforts for Imran's hospital. She said that she was prepared to travel to other countries in the Middle East to help raise money there.

Arriving back at the house, Diana made her way to the Khans' guest room. Imran Khan appeared, and it was at this point that the two of them had a heart to heart, during which time she confided in him how much she wanted to marry Hasnat Khan. In Imran's mind there was no doubt. 'He was the man!'

20

'Tell Dr Hasnat to marry the Princess!'

June 1997 was an extremely busy month for Diana. Three days into it she attended a performance of *Swan Lake* by the English National Ballet at the invitation of Mohamed Fayed, and three days later there were rumours of romance with another Pakistani – a fifty-eight-year-old businessman, Gulu Lalvani, who Diana had been photographed dancing with at Annabel's nightclub until two in the morning. Hasnat had been angered by the reports, so much so he had refused to speak to Diana for several days, and she resorted to calling Professor Jawad in Lahore to ask him to smooth things over between them.

Diana attended preview parties for the sale of her dresses in both London and New York. As another part of her PR campaign for the auction, she appeared on the cover of *Vanity Fair*. A two-and-a-half-page article was titled 'Diana Reborn', and showed the Princess with a new tousled look, prompting Richard Kay to ask in the *Daily Mail* whether, at last, *this* was the *real* Diana.

Diana was engrossed in her landmines campaign, making speeches in London and Washington on behalf of the Red Cross. After a meeting at the White House with Hillary Clinton, she flew to New York on 19 June to see Mother Teresa, who walked hand in hand with Diana through the tough streets of the Bronx where the two hugged, kissed and prayed together.

Two days later on Saturday 21 June 1997, almost a month after she had returned from her trip to Pakistan, Diana again drove herself in her BMW to Omar and Jane's house in Stratford-upon-Avon. Eleven members of Hasnat's family were flying over from Pakistan, and she was eager as ever to see them and particularly Appa.

Diana arrived at the house around ten in the morning, casually dressed in jeans, to find that some of the family, including three of the young children, had already arrived. After relaxing over a coffee with everyone it was decided that she would take the children shopping at the local Tesco supermarket. They were all incredibly excited about being allowed inside her BMW. Diana even had a television in the car, which they thought was really cool.

When they arrived at the supermarket, Diana grabbed a trolley, and swung into action. Soban, the youngest of the children, was sitting at the helm of the trolley as Diana negotiated the aisles at top speed. But it wasn't as easy as driving the BMW. She was going so fast she banged into a huge stack of baked beans, and they went flying; one of the cans burst open on the floor.

Shoppers were doing double takes and saying to each other, 'Is that really Princess Di?'

The children helped hide her identity, and to anyone who asked, they said, 'No, it isn't Lady Diana; this is Sharon!'

The children say that Diana was 'running and bumping into things'. But they loved it. 'We had a blast,' they all say. The children were amazed that Diana was acting so 'cool' and so 'common'. They loved the fact that she didn't act at all like a princess, but just like one of them. 'It was as if she was our cousin, one of us.'

Diana bought the children sweets, crisps and drinks. The man at the checkout asked 'Are you Diana?' and she said, 'No, of course not. Do I look like Diana? That's really nice.' But according to the children all the shoppers realized in the end that it really had been Diana, and everyone was waving at them as they left the car park.

On her return to the house, another part of the family had arrived in Stratford. This time it was Aunt Maryam, her husband Salahuddin Khan and their three youngsters. They hardly had a chance to say 'Hello' before the second contingent of children asked for a repeat performance of the Tesco trip, and Diana duly obliged.

Maryam is Appa's youngest daughter, and although she is Hasnat's aunt the two are around the same age and grew up together on the family estate in Jhelum.

She is of diminutive stature, and belongs to the efficient, organized, 'on the ball' school, keen to make sure that no time is ever wasted, turning up on the dot for appointments, and fretting in case she might be late. Nonetheless she always has the time to listen to problems, being generous hearted, warm and loyal in her attention to those close to her.

Her husband Salahuddin, a cousin of Imran Khan, loves a game of golf over cricket and has an irrepressible sense of humour. He is not known for hiding his opinion even if it causes upset on occasion; yet being blunt also makes him open, honest and thoroughly approachable.

After her forays to the supermarket, Diana flopped down in a chair and chatted with Maryam about the auction of her dresses, which was due to take place in New York four days later. Maryam thought it was a wonderful decision to have taken, and joked with Diana that it was a pity nothing would fit *her*.

Diana told her that each outfit was a reminder of her days as the wife of the heir to the throne, and selling her wardrobe was like shedding an old identity. She laughed and told Maryam she 'didn't need those things any more'.

After lunch Diana washed the dishes with the help of one of the Khan children; this was despite vehement protests from the family that the dirty plates and pans could all go into the dishwasher. Diana said, 'God has given us lovely hands and we should make use of them.'

Afterwards, the dishes needed to be put up on a rack, which Diana straightaway offered to do, as she was 'taller than anyone else' there.

The afternoon wore on, and Diana told them it was actually Prince William's fifteenth birthday that day, and that she was looking forward to seeing her boys again for the holidays. She said she'd love to take the Khan girls to Kensington Palace for a week, promising, 'I'll make ladies out of you!' Professor Jawad's wife, Uzma, retorted, 'How can you teach them to be true ladies when you haven't tuned out to be a lady yourself!' Obviously the story of the wild fling in the supermarket had got around.

Diana left late in the afternoon. Professor Jawad Khan needed to go to London for a meeting, so she offered to give him a lift. Diana asked jokingly, 'Wouldn't you like to drive my new tinted-glass BMW 750, complete with a Princess?' Jawad replied in like tone, 'Well, if we get a speeding ticket, I would give it to you!'

Before they set off Uzma gave her a present of a string of pearls. Diana promised she would never take them off. Uzma said, 'Oh, but you've got so much jewellery.' Diana said, 'Yes, but these have been given to me with so much love and affection.'

A week later, on 28 June, Hasnat arrived in Stratford to see his relatives. He appeared to be going through internal torment, wrestling with his wishes and desires, and his deep concerns about the question of marriage to Diana. It wasn't just that the press was causing Hasnat anxiety; his family says it was also the fact that Diana was a Princess and he felt he didn't always want to be in her shadow.

As always, conversations turned to the question of why Hasnat was still single. The family, in particular his mother, back in Lahore, felt that as he was now thirty-seven years old it was time he 'settled down'.

From everything people who know him say, it is clear that Hasnat Khan adores children, and would dearly like to have his own family.

He was loved by the most famous woman of the modern age; he knew it, his family knew it, and many others back in Pakistan knew it. But still he did not feel comfortable at the prospect of marrying somebody from such a different world.

For many Muslims, of course, the idea of a marriage between Khan and Diana would have been the dream match – a Muslim married to the mother of a future King of Great Britain. For Pakistan, in particular, such a marriage would have been a matter of huge national pride, and Hasnat was feeling that maybe others were wishing such a marriage on him for their own reasons. Sources close to the family say he was also uncomfortable with the idea of a marriage just for the sake of his country; he wanted a marriage to be for himself and his family, not for anybody else.

In Chelsea where Hasnat lives there is a corner shop, which is owned by a Pakistani family. Of course, everyone in the street knew Dr Hasnat lived where he did, and that Diana used to visit him there. The owner of the shop would tell any of Hasnat's visitors who happened to pop in for groceries, 'Tell Dr Hasnat to marry the Princess!' Asked why, he would say it would be 'a name for Pakistan all over the world!' It was this kind of opinion, which he knew was widely shared, that made Hasnat so uncomfortable.

However, reliable sources say that at the beginning of the summer Hasnat confided in at least one close relative that he was in love with Diana and he wanted to marry her. He had been very clear on this point. Another source says Hasnat was caught between a rock and a hard place, that it was very agonizing battling between what he wanted to do and what he was expected to do, there was no way through it. It was a conflict of cultures, religion, customs; everything was so different. And she was not an ordinary woman, she was Princess Diana from the Royal Family.

It was a desperate set of circumstances. Even though Diana had been to Pakistan to meet his parents, Hasnat had not yet asked his father whether he could marry her. After three failed arranged engagements, his mother would have been on the back foot, so if her son had asked her opinion about marrying Diana she might not have dared to say no. At the same time Hasnat did not want to do anything to upset his parents.

In fact he had already denied to his mother that he had any romantic interest in Diana. This was in the summer of 1996, in the presence of his Uncle Ashfaq. Hasnat's mother had asked her son outright what was going on with Diana, and he had denied his interest in her. But the version he gave to his mother clearly conflicted with the feelings in his own heart, at least as he described them to others in the family. It was an illustration of how important to him his mother's feelings were.

So by the end of June 1997 Hasnat had still not asked his parents about marrying Diana. In turn they had not said 'No', as they had never been asked. Yet Hasnat loved Diana and wanted to marry her, so he was torn in two. He wanted to please his parents and to do right by himself and Diana. He found himself unable to take the big step.

While Hasnat was wrestling with such thoughts, in New York the sale of seventy-nine of Diana's dresses on 25 June had proved to be a huge success, raising over two million pounds for charity from the auction at Christie's. One of the dresses had been successfully bid for by a London-based photographer called Jason Fraser. He had gone to New York for *Paris Match* to bid $65,000 dollars for Lot 4 – a knee-length black cocktail dress – the idea being that the French magazine would hold a competition and offer the dress as first prize. It was several years since the Princess had had any contact with Fraser, but she noticed him outside the auction and exchanged a cordial nod. Fraser didn't know it then but he would soon be seeing a lot more of Diana.

A friend of hers recounts how terribly hot it was in New York that day, a stifling ninety-five degrees. When it was all over, Diana flew back to England and of course she met the usual grey skies and drizzle. But as soon as she was back at Kensington Palace, she took off her suit, changed into jeans and a little top and ran out into the Palace gardens. She just danced in the rain, getting soaking wet in the process. Afterwards she ran back inside and told her staff, 'I feel much better now.'

She said later that it was almost as if something had lifted, if only for a moment. Diana felt free, no longer the bird in the gilded cage, no longer lonely, she had let something go inside, and just for that moment it seemed the self-doubt had disappeared. For once her life seemed to be opening up to endless possibilities.

The whole summer stretched ahead of her, and Diana had already been busy making plans for the early part of the season. But her plans were still overshadowed by frustration.

Hasnat Khan's soul searching was leading nowhere. He had failed to commit himself on the question of marriage, although he must have known how desperate Diana was to move forward.

July 1997 was a turbulent month in the hearts and minds of both of them. Events would pressure Hasnat into making a decision whose ramifications he could never have imagined.

By the end of the month, Diana had begun a fateful affair with Dodi Fayed, the son of Mohamed Fayed. In stark contrast to the secrecy that had surrounded her relationship with Hasnat, her romance with Dodi was trumpeted throughout the world.

21

'Tell Hasnat I'm coming back'

On 11 July 1997 a Harrods helicopter picked up Diana and her two sons from Kensington Palace, and flew them out to lunch to the Fayed Elizabethan mansion, Barrow Green Court, at Oxted in Surrey, before moving on to Stansted airport, where they boarded a private jet to Nice. From there they were driven to the small harbour of St Laurent-du-Var where they boarded a luxury yacht called the *Jonikal*.

Aboard the *Jonikal* they sailed along the coast of the French Riviera towards the millionaires' playground of St Tropez, where the Harrods boss owned a villa.

Diana and the boys had been invited on holiday by Mohamed Fayed in late May, a few days after she returned from Lahore in Pakistan. The Princess had known Fayed for many years; he had been a friend of her late father Earl Spencer, and her stepmother Raine served on the board of Harrods International.

Fayed had asked Diana to spend holidays with him before, but she had always refused. This year was different. She was in a state of turmoil after her relationship with Hasnat seemed to have reached an impasse. She needed a distraction, and when the opportunity arose to escape from Kensington Palace Diana grabbed it. In early June she decided to accept Fayed's offer.

This was the first summer since her divorce, and Diana's primary concern was to give the children a good holiday. She thought William and Harry would enjoy themselves in the company of the four young Fayed children – Karim, Jasmine, Camilla and Omar. Her need for privacy had been assured by Fayed's tight security arrangements around the villa Castel Ste Thérèse, which sits in a ten-acre estate high on the cliffs, complete with its own small Mediterranean beach.

Fayed had bought the fifteen-million-pound yacht, the *Jonikal*, with the specific aim of impressing his Royal guest. Now she and her sons spent their days either swimming off the *Jonikal* or lounging by the pool at the villa. As long as Diana stayed inside the estate she would be guaranteed her privacy, but the minute they ventured down to the private beach to go jet-skiing, sailing or scuba diving they became targets for the paparazzi, who, less than twenty-four hours after Diana had left London, had arrived en masse at the Côte d'Azur and uncovered the secret location of her holiday.

Three days after her arrival, on 14 July, utterly fed up with the intrusion, Diana took matters into her own hands and gave an impromptu press conference at sea for the British press. She said, 'You are going to get a big surprise with the next thing I do.'

What did Diana mean by this? If the answer to that question was known with any certainty, many of the events that were to take place over the course of the next six weeks might seem clearer. But what is sure is that she had something up her sleeve; Diana was planning something, and would be 'using' the press along the way.

At the same 'press conference' she hinted that she might leave Britain one day, because she was finding the endless media scrutiny so hard to bear. She said that the attention was embarrassing, and she was afraid her sons' holiday was being spoiled.

Mohamed Fayed sensed a loneliness and a longing for companionship in Diana, and three days into the holiday he thought he could provide the answer. On the same day as the impromptu press conference, Dodi Fayed, who was in Paris with his model girlfriend Kelly Fisher celebrating Bastille Day, received a phone call from his father requesting him to join them immediately and help to entertain the Princess.

Dodi was forty-two years old, and was planning to marry his American model girlfriend just three weeks later in Los Angeles, where Fayed had already bought a seven-million dollar, five-acre estate for them in Malibu's Paradise Cove. The estate had once been owned by singer and actress Julie Andrews. Ever mindful of doing his father's bidding, Dodi set off to St Tropez, leaving his thirty-one-year-old fiancée behind.

Dodi, or Emad, meaning 'someone to depend on', was born 15 April 1955, in Alexandria in Egypt. His mother was Samira Khashoggi, sister of the arms dealer Adnan Khashoggi. In 1956, his parents split up after only two years of marriage and Fayed was granted custody of his son, consistent with Egyptian law.

Dodi had led a rather rootless existence. 'Home' for the young Fayed boy had varied between a boarding school near Gstaad in Switzerland, holiday houses in France and Egypt, or yachts that drifted in and out of various Mediterranean ports. By the age of fifteen he had his own apartment in London's Park Lane, a chauffeured Rolls Royce and a bodyguard. At eighteen he enrolled at Sandhurst, the British Army's Officer Training School, but decided military life was not for him.

Life as a playboy and film producer did beckon though. He invested in the musical *Breaking Glass* (1980), and the films *Chariots of Fire* (1981) and *The World According to Garp* (1982). He had once been married, in 1984, to the model Suzanne Gregard, but it had lasted only ten months.

When he arrived in St Tropez at the behest of his father it was not the first time Diana and Dodi had met. They had previously encountered each other at a polo match in July 1986 as Diana's marriage to Charles was starting to disintegrate. In 1992, Diana had taken her sons to the London film première of the Steven Spielberg film *Hook*, and met him again. Diana got to know him better in the spring of 1997, when stepmother Raine brought them together at a dinner party. But that was all; they had rubbed shoulders a few times, during which there had been no obvious magic between them, and so it might have continued had not Diana been in need of company in the wake of all the frustrations with Hasnat.

Dodi arrived at the *Jonikal* accompanied by his bodyguard Trevor Rees-Jones on the evening of 14 July. Trevor's friend and colleague, Alexander Wingfield, known to his friends as 'Kez', was already there, based at the villa.

During five days spent on board the *Jonikal*, Diana and Dodi enjoyed many close conversations. They were both from broken homes, each having been separated at an early age from their mothers, and both had suffered deep insecurities as a result.

To those that knew the history of her recent attachments, Dodi was consistent with Diana's penchant for Eastern and Middle Eastern friends. The Fayeds were Egyptian not Asian, but like the Khans they were Muslim. When she holidayed with the Fayeds Diana experienced that warm, compelling embrace of a large family that she so cherished, and which was so different from Establishment families of her early experience.

She told her friend Lady Elsa Bowker, 'I've never been so spoiled, so loved; it's wonderful to feel that warmth.'

To her friend Rosa Monckton she said, 'It's bliss.'[1]

Unlike Hasnat Khan, Dodi had no daily responsibilities, and so he could afford to devote all the time in the world to Diana; that is, when he wasn't shuttling between boats. On 16 July, Kelly Fisher flew down from Paris to join Dodi, but instead of being included in the main party, Fisher stayed on another Fayed yacht, the *Sakara*. Over the next two days Dodi yo-yoed between the villa during the daytime and the yacht, to be with Fisher, at night.

1 *Requiem: Diana Princess of Wales 1961–1997*

In terms of the timing, Diana's meeting with Dodi was an auspicious distraction, as one of the things that was uppermost in her mind was Camilla Parker Bowles's fiftieth birthday party on 18 July at Highgrove, the Gloucestershire home she first shared with Charles after their marriage. Despite their public acrimony, Charles remained an important figure in her life, but her newfound self-confidence meant he had lost his hold over her. However, she could still sometimes be unnerved by the thought of Camilla being together with Charles.

According to Debbie Frank, 'Dodi was somebody who came into Diana's life in that July when she really needed an out. She needed to get away from her feelings of despair that were coming back about Camilla and the possibility that Camilla and Charles would be together.'

On that morning of 18 July the tabloids were full of photographs of Diana swimming, diving and riding behind Harry on his jet-ski. After nearly two years spent ducking and diving the press when she had been with Hasnat Khan, it was a relief to be able to be seen in the open with someone. Clearly she wanted to be spotted, and she actually wanted to be more public about getting on with her life.

On 20 July, Diana and the boys flew back to London on a Harrods private jet. That evening William and Harry went to Balmoral, and Diana knew it would be another month before she would see them again. The next day Dodi sent Diana huge quantities of pink roses and arranged delivery of his very first gift – a solid gold Panther watch worth almost seven thousand pounds.

Friends say that Diana cared very little for the shower of material gifts that Dodi was to bestow on her. She chatted casually with her friend Roberto Devorik about the gifts. 'I think she was fascinated with Dodi, and the culture of Dodi. I said to her, "My God, I hear you are full of presents and things", and she said, "Well, you know that's not what I like the most in my life."'

On 22 July Diana was one of the guests at the funeral service in Milan for murdered fashion designer Gianni Versace. Diana was sitting next to rock singer Elton John, and was seen comforting him.

Four days later on Saturday 26 July, Diana travelled to Paris for a hastily arranged secret rendezvous with Dodi. She stayed at the Ritz, Fayed's hotel on the famous Place Vendôme, which the Harrods boss had purchased in 1979. The six-thousand-pounds-a-night Imperial Suite had been set aside for her.

Dodi picked her up at the heliport near the Eiffel Tower and took her to see the Windsor villa, where the Duke and Duchess of Windsor had lived together in exile from 1953 until his death in 1972, before Diana and Dodi dined at the three-star Lucas Carton restaurant.

After sleeping alone at the hotel, she took breakfast with Dodi, before leaving again on Sunday 27 July for London.

Diana had made few plans for August, and could see a lonely month stretching ahead of her. So when she was invited on a second six-day cruise to Corsica and Sardinia aboard the *Jonikal* on 31 July, she accepted. Only this time she was to be alone with Dodi.

Back in London Hasnat Khan had been struggling with his feelings over whether or not he should – or could – marry Diana. Clearly, overcoming the resistance he believed his mother would feel was an issue, whether or not she would ever articulate those feelings to him. Left to Appa, on the other hand, the decision about a marriage would almost certainly have been favourable. But Appa was his grandmother, not his mother.

At the beginning of July, various members of his family were still in England, on their extended vacation, and from time to time he would see them and talk to them. It was during this time that he finally made a decision as to what to do about Diana.

Hasnat was still in love with Diana, and very much wanted to marry her, but the underlying anxieties were still there, and Diana knew perfectly well that he had reservations; he had laid out some of his concerns to her about the enormous disparity between them; not just in cultural but in financial terms too, reportedly saying that his take home salary was about eighteen hundred to two thousand pounds a month. Could she live with that, and live in his one-bedroom flat?

Although Pathans are at the upper echelons of Pakistani society, it appears that Khan also had reservations concerning marriage to someone of Diana's status and station, and particularly to someone with a permanent link through her sons to the British Royal Family.

His idea of the perfect marriage would also include being able to take it for granted that his wife would be there to look after the whole family, and would always be around when his parents came to visit. The doctor was basically a family man who needed a relationship which maintained the closeness and comfort of the family, so that whoever visited him would be welcome, and there would be warmth in the house – not a celebrity house, but an ordinary down-to-earth place.

Hasnat was torn, agonizing between what he wanted to do and how he felt, and what he was expected to do and the realities of marrying the mother of a future King of Great Britain.

At the beginning of July, Salahuddin Khan, husband of Aunt Maryam and uncle to Hasnat, left Omar and Jane's in Stratford to go and stay with Hasnat in his London flat for a few days.

Salahuddin had gone alone to London so that he could get on with some work, away from the distraction of the rest of the family in Stratford. One day, when he was alone in the flat and busy at work, the telephone rang. Hasnat had already left for work and would be away all day. Salahuddin picked up the receiver; it was Diana. They exchanged greetings, then Diana asked to speak with Hasnat, and Salahuddin told her he wasn't in.

Then she said, 'Tell Hasnat I'm coming back on the (she specified a date a few days hence which Salahuddin can't remember but it would appear to be the twentieth), and ask him to give me a call in the evening.' It appeared that Diana was still actively engaged in the relationship.

When Hasnat Khan arrived home, Salahuddin relayed the message. Diana was still in love with Hasnat Khan at this stage, and even in July, according to sources close to Doctor Khan's family, Hasnat himself had not given up the idea of marrying her; this is illustrated, according to the source, by the fact that he was talking of asking his parents to come over to London so that he could discuss with them the question of marriage.

It was clearly a big issue in his mind, and the fact that so many of his relatives were in Britain at that time perhaps made it even more so. Their presence in the country would doubtless have made him think more about the ramifications of marriage to Diana for his family in Pakistan.

Unsure what to do, in mid-July Hasnat finally confided his feelings to a trusted confidante. Pakistani sources confirm the advice he received in return was simple; he should end the affair and get on with his life.

He took the advice.

Hasnat Khan had reached his decision, and at some point after Diana had returned from the south of France on 20 July Khan relayed that decision to Diana, who must have been totally devastated.

On 2 August various relatives were due to return home to Pakistan. Final farewells were made, and sources close to the family say that Hasnat was handed some cards, goodbye, thank you things, that the children had made for Diana, and wanted him to give to her. Hasnat replied he wasn't able to give them to her because, 'I am not seeing her any more.' He didn't elaborate further on this point, but said the cards would have to be posted.

So by early August, the relationship, in his mind, at least, was over, and he had told Diana of his decision.

However, until now it has always been assumed by the press that Diana and Hasnat had parted long before, in early summer or even sooner. Based on this assumption, the subsequent relationship between Diana and Dodi took on a greater significance than it ever deserved.

Speculation about Dodi and Diana has been based on a fallacy. The fact is that Hasnat was very much in the picture until late July, and Diana was to remain in touch with the Khan family until the end. This puts an entirely different complexion on the events that were to take place in the last four weeks of her life.

The final drama began to unfold at the end of July 1997. Diana had been told by the man she loved that they must stop seeing each other. However, she was not about to take the rejection lying down.

She was already formulating a plan.

22

Anatomy of a Kiss

Following her secret rendezvous in Paris with Dodi Fayed, Diana flew back to London. It was Sunday 27 July, and she had already made arrangements to see him again the following Thursday for a six-day cruise aboard the *Jonikal*.

By now Hasnat Khan had told Diana that he wanted to end their relationship. Whether she really believed this was his true intention or not determines what drove her over the next four weeks. Khan had stopped seeing her on at least one previous occasion, following the Sydney article, and it is unlikely that she would have accepted a 'No' as final this time.

Diana must have been running through the options, such as they were. Any self-respecting Mills and Boon reader knows that to win her man back, the heroine must make him jealous, and jealousy was certainly a weapon in Diana's armoury that she had used before.

Two days into the *Jonikal* cruise, on Saturday 2 August, a few hours before Hasnat Khan was to see off members of his family, an aircraft carrying a single Italian photographer – a 'paparazzo' – touched down in Sardinia. In itself this was an unusual event; the paparazzi normally end up hunting in the same territory, but this was one man on a solo mission with no competition.

His name was Mario Brenna. Then forty years old, and based in Milan, he had been on the paparazzo scene for many years. The word 'paparazzi' nowadays conjures up all sorts of negative images; yet Brenna was and is highly respected throughout the twin worlds of fashion and Mediterranean high society. Before the murder of Gianni Versace, he was the fashion designer's personal photographer and as such was allowed to shoot photographs at Versace's parties and syndicate them to fashion and gossip magazines all over the world.

But that was all in the past; less than three weeks before, the designer had been murdered, and among other notable friends at his funeral in Milan on 22 July was Princess Diana.

Now he was in pursuit of the *Jonikal*, trying to snap pictures of Diana and Dodi aboard what the journalists were to later refer to as the 'love boat' as it cruised the Mediterranean.

Diana was back amidst the sumptuous luxury of the *Jonikal*, to all appearances without a care in the world. The vessel was one hundred and eighty feet long, with twelve sleeping cabins and it normally put to sea with a crew of sixteen. The yacht had two deck levels, three living rooms, a dining room, an outdoor lounge area, two kitchens, a sundeck, and even a helipad. Soaking up the sun, Diana and Dodi would read sections of *The Times* and *Daily Mail* to each other.[1]

Rene Delorm, Dodi's Moroccan-born butler, who had joined the couple on the cruise wondered what they found to talk about for hours on end. Diana, of course, was also busy on her mobile phone, as ever giving a running commentary on her life and her thoughts to friends.

But although Diana, luxuriating aboard the *Jonikal*, was obviously enjoying Dodi's company, a fact that has never been revealed before is that she was *not* ignorant of the lurking presence of a 'paparazzo'. The fact that Mario Brenna was hovering

1 Rene Delorm, *Diana & Dodi: A Love Story*

close by waiting for the right moment was no accident, but part of a wider plan.

Reliable sources say that Brenna received his information about the *Jonikal* from a colleague in London – another photographer, Jason Fraser, who Diana had spotted at the auction of her dresses in New York.

Thirty-three-year-old Fraser, whose career selling pictures to local newspapers began at the tender age of twelve, once covered news and even conflict areas, such as the Middle East and Northern Ireland. He shot sessions with Margaret Thatcher and John Major before switching to the more lucrative world of showbiz and glamour.

A classy, impressive, super-focused operator, with a no-nonsense attitude and multilingual ability to boot, Fraser says most of the material he shoots is taken with the subject's consent.

Fraser was known to have been heavily tipped-off on many occasions by Dr James Colthurst between the years 1989 and 1991. Colthurst was the man who recorded Diana's recollections for Andrew Morton which ultimately formed the basis of *Diana, Her True Story,* and the tip-offs Colthurst had been given to pass on to Fraser were coming directly from Diana. Such tip-offs enabled Fraser to break news about her relationships at the time.

According to the same sources, in the last six weeks of Diana's life, Fraser once again had access to her circle; indeed he clearly enjoyed better access than anyone else.

The sequence of events that was to lead to one of the most dramatic images of Diana ever taken began on 30 July, shortly after her return from the secret Paris weekend. Although there have been theories surrounding the 'KISS' pictures before, no one has been able to demonstrate until now that the pictures were not only orchestrated but that it was Diana herself who was behind it all.

Without warning Fraser received a phone call. This came from someone particularly close and 'loyal' to Diana. Dodi was not aware of the plan for the proposed pictures Brenna was subsequently to take.

The caller gave Fraser information that Diana and Dodi had gone away together, and told him which yacht they were on. The photographer was given to understand there wouldn't be any complaints about the photographs being taken of the two of them together. Fraser himself refuses to comment saying only that, 'I was receiving information, but under no circumstances will I ever reveal who my sources are.'

Fraser discussed the information with Mario Brenna, whose expert knowledge of the Italian Riviera made him best placed to act.

The exact locations and sequence of events surrounding the 'KISS' pictures have never been previously revealed either, and are disclosed here for the first time.

Shortly after arriving on 2 August, Brenna spotted the *Jonikal* moored off Cala di Volpe in north-east Sardinia. He saw a blonde woman on the telephone as he circled the yacht in his powerful inflatable boat two hundred yards away, but was not absolutely sure it was Diana. For the next six hours from one o'clock in the afternoon to seven o'clock in the evening he continued to observe the boat, but took no pictures. It was now sunset, and he decided to wait until the following morning before attempting to take any photographs. Early the next morning, at seven o'clock, Sunday 3 August, Brenna returned to where the boat was moored and hung around for the next five hours. Now sure the blonde woman was Diana, he was waiting for the right opportunity to get a decent shot; so far she had spent all the time on the phone and then disappeared below deck. A phone call alerting the photographer to another story about five miles away resulted in Brenna taking a short trip to Porto Rotondo to check the matter out. To his dismay, two hours later when he returned to Cala di Volpe, the *Jonikal* had disappeared. Crestfallen, he rang Fraser with an update, at which point the London photographer toyed with the idea of flying out there himself, but Brenna reassured him he had the situation under control.

Whoever was controlling events was an arch manipulator. For

although Brenna and Fraser were acting on a tip-off, there was only a certain amount of information being relayed – just enough to still have the photographers guessing and give the appearance of a chase. The end result: to make it look as if it wasn't a tip-off at all.

That Sunday evening Brenna received welcome information from a girlfriend to say that Diana and Dodi had been seen walking around the shops in Porto Cervo, so the photographer knew the boat must be close by. The following morning, Monday 4 August, Brenna woke at six o'clock and began to look for the vessel in his powerboat. His luck was in. Mario Brenna locked onto the boat once again and this time he moved into action. The *Jonikal* set sail for Corsica at ten o'clock, and Brenna, determined not to let it out of his sight, followed it travelling at a speed of 20 nautical miles an hour. Between Sardinia and Corsica the *Jonikal* stopped at Isola Piana at the southern tip of Corsica, and Diana and Dodi got into a tender and went for a swim in the very shallow waters. It was here that the first few pictures of the 'KISS' set were snapped.

Then the couple set off on their own in the tender which had an outboard motor, and after a while they stopped the motor and drifted into the shallow waters around Ille Cavallo. Brenna had meanwhile bumped into some Italian friends holidaying in the area with their families, and had asked to join them on their boat. It was a perfect cover. As Diana and Dodi sunbathed on the tender Brenna shot a sequence of photographs of them from as close as twenty yards.

Diana had a sixth sense when a camera was trained on her. 'She had an amazing instinct when a camera was pointed at her. She just knew,' said one of her close contacts. Indeed, looking at what subsequently came to be called the 'KISS' pictures, there is one shot where Diana appears to be looking straight at the camera. The straps of her black and white swimsuit are dangling down around her elbows provocatively; it is almost as if Diana had sensed Brenna was there taking the pictures, and yet she is making no attempt to hide her face, which was so often her immediate reaction on being accosted by unwelcome photographers. Instead she carries on undisturbed by her apparent realization that the pictures were being taken.

An hour later, at lunchtime, Diana and Dodi went back to the *Jonikal*, and Brenna continued shadowing the vessel for the rest of the afternoon. It now moored at Punte de Sprono, and Brenna tried to get near the *Jonikal* in his own smaller boat, but decided he was too visible so went back ashore. There, climbing on to some rocks, he attached an ultra powerful Canon 800mm lens to the camera and waited. Around five o'clock that afternoon the couple happened to be standing on the deck of the boat. Brenna snapped a further sequence of pictures from a range of about 500 yards. These were to become the famous set of four 'KISS' pictures. They showed Diana in a red floral swimsuit with her arms around a barechested Dodi, the two of them locked in tender embrace. Although the shots turned out to be fairly grainy, as Brenna was operating at the limits of technical capability, they were about to ignite a firestorm.

Having completed his mission, Brenna caught the first flight to Paris and immediately went to process the pictures before boarding a plane to London. Arriving at Jason Fraser's home, the two of them laid out the pictures on the kitchen floor and toasted their success. By Wednesday 6 August, word had started to leak out that pictures of Diana and Dodi kissing passionately were available, and by Thursday Fleet Street was in a frenzy. Fraser was receiving phone calls at the rate of thirty an hour, and picture editors were turning up on his doorstep saying they were desperate to discuss the photographs with him. A furious bidding war erupted, which culminated in the *Sunday Mirror* paying a quarter of a million pounds for the first rights to run three-quarters of the pictures; the *Sun* and the *Daily Mail* paid a hundred thousand pounds each for second rights to run the full set.

What broke the following Sunday, August 10, was not just a standard front page spread, but the classic case of a picture 'telling a thousand words'. This was not just a 'snog', but true 'romance'.

The hazy pictures showed Diana and Dodi kissing and would be held as 'proof' that the two of them were in love: 'Locked in her lover's arms, the Princess finds happiness at last' ran the subhead under the two-inch-thick headline 'THE KISS'.

Later that same month, in the last ten days of Diana's life, Fraser accumulated a further six front pages worth of pictures of the Princess for the UK newspaper market alone.

At ten minutes to ten on the evening of 21 August, eleven days after the 'KISS' pictures had been published, Diana and Dodi arrived in the south of France for the start of their second cruise together. They had flown from Stansted airport to Nice in the Fayed jet, and from there had been transferred by Range Rover and Mercedes to a deserted corner of the port of St Laurent-du-Var. Fraser was already waiting on the pier at St Laurent-du-Var along with two colleagues from France's leading showbusiness photo-agency, Eliot Press.

Despite the fact there were literally hundreds of other sharp-eyed and financially motivated members of the press after them, somehow Fraser was always the one to get the picture. He would be in position at the same time as, or even before, the couple arrived anywhere. On the evening of 21 August he had been in position for two hours before Diana and Dodi had arrived at the small French port.

It was simply not possible for him to know the couple's movements with such a degree of accuracy unless he had been tipped off.

The couple were snapped under cover of darkness as they boarded a boat that was to take them to the *Jonikal*. There is a genuine look of surprise on Dodi's face at the realization that their hush-hush holiday plans had somehow been uncovered. Diana is seen looking the other way.

Over the following eight days, Fraser was able to take all of the pictures he wanted of the couple on board the *Jonikal,* as it cruised from St Laurent-du-Var to St Tropez to St Jean-Cap-Ferrat, overnighting in Monaco before sailing on to Portofino and Sardinia.

Sources say that, in contrast to the events leading up to the original 'KISS' pictures when Fraser was being tipped off *only* by an intermediary, by 24 August – three days into the second cruise – the information Fraser was receiving was also coming from a more direct source.

It is understood that Fraser, who must have known who the real source was, was totally thrown off course when the next call came not from the intermediary but actually from Diana herself. Fraser realized a turning point had been reached, and after 24 August this proved to be another way in which he was to receive his information. The conversations with him on his mobile phone ran along the lines of, 'Are you there? Are you getting this? What did you get just now?'

The boat had been moored at the exclusive Italian resort of Portofino when the famous sequence of Diana and Dodi canoodling on a bed of yellow cushions on the upper deck of the Jonikal was taken. Diana was wearing a blue swimsuit, having changed from a yellow costume, and sometimes had a yellow towel round her waist. Dodi wore a pair of yellow shorts and is seen stroking Diana's face and shoulders. The following Monday morning, 25 August, as the photographer was apparently in his hotel room, sources say Diana called up after the pictures had been published and even asked why they had been so grainy.

Sources also suggest that whereas only Diana knew about the first set of 'KISS' pictures, in the last few days both parties knew the pictures were being taken.

What this indicates is that towards the end, Diana and Dodi

both knew what was going on; both wanted to show off the relationship – but for very different reasons! Dodi so that he could boast to the world he was with its most famous woman, and fulfil his father's wishes; Diana, it seems, had her own quite separate reasons.

Fraser refuses to say how he was able to take the photographs so easily. He will only acknowledge that he was receiving accurate, precise information.

The process of taking pictures continued until 28 August at which point Fraser was told there were enough pictures and no more were required. The photographer was therefore not in Paris when the fatal accident happened.

The 'KISS' pictures, and those that followed later in the month, had obviously been deliberately orchestrated. If so they can only have been designed to send a message.

It is a fact that Diana manipulated the press; she had a history of using pictures to send potent messages. She did it in February 1992 in front of the Taj Mahal, and later that year in front of the pyramids at Giza in Egypt, to name but two occasions. She also knew from long experience how best to avoid the press when she didn't want her picture taken.

Her method of operating usually involved a trusted friend or go-between passing on information to the press. This was often James Colthurst until 1992, and then Simone Simmons until March 1997. She would also use a favoured press reporter as a conduit for news stories, often Andrew Morton, or in later years, Richard Kay.

All the evidence confirms Diana herself was the source for the tip off for the 'KISS' pictures.

So she had to have a motive for those pictures being taken. It seems apparent from the timing that there can only have been one reason: to flush out Hasnat Khan's true feelings in order to try and win him back.

* * *

Somewhere between 20 July and 31 July following the advice of his trusted confidant, Hasnat Khan had told Diana that the relationship was over.

Diana would have been in a delicate state of mind anyway; on 15 July she learned that her friend Gianni Versace had been murdered by a gunman stalking him outside his Miami Beach palazzo, and on 19 July she heard that Sir James Goldsmith, father of Jemima, and the man who had given her behind-the-scenes help with her divorce, had also died, in Paris. Now to be told by the man she loved and wanted to marry and spend the rest of her life with that everything was over between them must have been devastating.

If she had been told this shortly after her arrival back to London from Milan on 22 July then it is little wonder that Diana agreed to go for a secret weekend with Dodi on 26 July – it would have meant an escape from the heartache she must have felt.

The timing of the tip-off to Jason Fraser, which according to sources was 30 July, allows us to conclude that Diana was thinking of using the holiday to send a powerful message to Hasnat Khan.

In all her relationships, Diana liked to be the one in control. This time it was different, this time it was Khan telling her it was all over between them. According to Lady Elsa Bowker, Diana had pursued Khan so vigorously partly because he seemed so unobtainable – the more distant he was, the more she wanted him. Now when it seemed he might be slipping away from her for ever, her desire to be with him had never been stronger, and she was doing everything she could to win him back.

But could her actions in engineering the 'KISS' pictures have been driven by revenge against Hasnat for letting her down? Roberto Devorik says, 'If you are asking me if she went out with him [Dodi] to revenge herself on another relationship – no way. No way. It was not in Diana's mentality to be like that, and she never did that before.'

Although Diana was not the sort of person to take revenge, she knew from past experience that stories in the press *could* result in an emotional response from Hasnat: the report from Sydney in November 1996 when she denied the relationship had upset Khan, and more pertinently the suggestion in the papers in June 1997 that there might be romance between her and Gulu Lalvani had caused Hasnat to cry foul.

Despite not being a demonstrative person when it came to his feelings, Hasnat Khan was not a shallow man either, and those close to him have observed that he said goodbye to Diana out of a sense of hopelessness rather than any loss of love. Diana knew, therefore, that despite Hasnat having been the one to end their relationship, pictures of her openly kissing another Muslim man might have resulted in outraged despair, and perhaps even provoked a jealousy that might have brought him back to her.

There is more evidence to illustrate Diana's approval of the kind of pictures that were being used, and the line that was being taken. Whereas it is apparent that Diana became very emotional, upset or just exercised about other graphic photographs, the 'KISS' photographs, probably the most dramatic images in her entire life, were greeted with no surprise whatsoever.

On 8 August 1997 Diana flew to Bosnia, as part of her continuing campaign to eliminate landmines. She took off from London in a private jet belonging to currency speculator George Soros, destined for Sarajevo.

Diana had been forced to scrap her original plans after the embarrassing disclosure that the President of the local Red Cross in Bosnia was the wife of accused war criminal Radavan Karadzic. However she quickly found new sponsors in the Land -mine Survivors Network, and in Norwegian People's Aid, two organizations dedicated to assisting victims of landmines.

While in Bosnia she was staying in private accommodation

with the Erikson family in the hills in Tuzla. None of the hotels in the area was deemed to be appropriate, and the family had been taking in lodgers from the Red Cross. Diana arrived, accompanied by two Scotland Yard police officers, her butler Paul Burrell, and the *Daily Telegraph* columnist, Lord Deedes.

Sandra Erikson, whose husband works for Norwegian People's Aid, remembers Diana standing at the bottom of her garden talking on the satellite phone frequently during this time. She remembers overhearing conversations that Diana was clearly having with Dodi Fayed. It was not really surprising that the two of them would be talking, as the 'KISS' had exploded in the press two days after she arrived in Bosnia, and the world's journalists were now in hot pursuit of her.

Although Diana was worried that the pictures may divert press attention away from the cause she was there to promote, she seemed curiously unconcerned about the appearance of her affair being made so public in the press.

On the flight back from Bosnia Diana was perusing the newspaper coverage. Maybe she was looking to see what they were saying about her visit, but she was totally unfazed by what was actually there in front of her. It was the 'KISS' image in full graphic detail, complete with editorial interpretation.

23

'Look here, I'm not for sale!'

So what of her relationship with Dodi? On 15 August Diana flew to Greece for a holiday with her friend Rosa Monckton. Rosa is a confident and articulate woman, married to Dominic Lawson, the editor of the *Sunday Telegraph*, and her grandfather, Walter Monckton, was once legal adviser to King Edward VIII, helping him write his famous abdication speech.

The two women had originally been booked on an Olympic Airways flight, but a couple of days before going, Diana rang Rosa to say that Dodi would prefer them to use the Fayed jet. On board the sumptuous aircraft Diana giggled, 'Look at all this, Rosa; isn't it awful?' as they sat in plush pink seats, with their feet disappearing into the green pile carpet decorated with pharaohs' heads.

It wasn't the only time during that trip that she brought up her dislike of material things. As Monckton writes in *Requiem*, Diana would feel very angry whenever Dodi would call and recite a list of presents he had purchased for her. 'That's not what I want, Rosa, it makes me uneasy. I don't want to be bought; I have everything I want. I just want someone to be there for me, to make me feel safe and secure.'

In Roberto Devorik's view, Diana was not someone for whom love must be signalled by the giving of presents or the buying of beautiful rings or watches. For her, love was about actions and feelings, and genuinely thinking about her. 'I knew Dodi,' says Devorik, 'he was an Oriental kind of guy, and they like to treat their women in a generous and flamboyant way. And Diana never felt comfortable with flamboyancy.'

According to Lady Bowker, Diana's reaction to the gifts was more abrupt. When Dodi persisted in saying, 'I'll give you this jewel . . . I'll give you this . . . I'll give you,' she turned around and snapped at him, 'Look here, I'm not for sale!'

Diana returned from Greece to London on 21 August, but flew out again that same evening from Stansted to Nice, for her second cruise with Dodi Fayed aboard the *Jonikal*. This time the trip was scheduled to last for ten days. As the boat cruised from St Laurent-du-Var to St Tropez to St Jean-Cap-Ferrat, to Monaco, Portofino and Sardinia, Jason Fraser continued to snap the set-up photographs that dominated the front page

The arguments that are said to support a Diana and Dodi marriage plan are basically threefold: that there was a proposal, that there was a ring, and that the couple found a house in which they wanted to live. The couple's movements have been closely analysed from every point of view, and prove nothing. Only closer examination of conversations that Diana had in the last weeks of her life can give evidence of what was happening in her own mind.

Ever the mobile phone junkie, Diana had maintained her cellular habits throughout her time on board the *Jonikal*. If Diana kept her friends in separate 'cubby holes' and compartments, to all of them that last August there was a consistent line that they each concur with as independent witnesses: as far as Diana was concerned Dodi was a summer romance and nothing more.

Although she undoubtedly enjoyed his company, and needed to submerge herself in somebody else's presence after her rejection by Hasnat Khan, Diana's conversations with her confidants in the last week of her life reveal evidence that she was neither in love with Dodi nor did she intend to marry him.

One of those confidants was someone who should have been on holiday with Diana during those last few days of her life. Diana had originally planned a late August holiday not in the French Riviera or Paris, but in Milan, with her friend Lana Marks.

South-African born Lana Marks had been introduced to Diana by the wife of the Brazilian ambassador to Washington, Lucia Flecha de Lima, in June 1996. Marks is an American accessory designer specializing in handbags and belts.

The idea was that she would attend various functions in America with Diana, hopefully allowing Diana to feel more comfortable because of the constant presence of a familiar face. The two women met privately at Kensington Palace in October 1996, and soon 'clicked', and it wasn't long before they were on the phone to each other an average of twice a week, although sometimes it was up to three times a day for forty-five minutes at a time.

Marks and Diana had often spoken about spending a little time away together, somewhere in Europe. Finally, in the summer of 1997, Diana managed to clear some space in her diary between 25 and 28 August. In anticipation of the trip, the Four Seasons hotel in Milan was booked for two nights. The two women planned to go to the opera at La Scala, before moving on to Lake Como for the final evening.

Flight tickets were booked, and everything was in place. However, on 24 July, Marks's father died suddenly after a heart attack, and she had to go to South Africa for his funeral. She rang Diana in early August deciding she would have to cancel the trip as things would take a while to sort out. So when the invitation for a second holiday with Dodi arose, Diana was not only able to accept but could extend it up till the last weekend in August because of the sudden space in her diary. Ironically, if the holiday with Marks had gone ahead Diana would in all likelihood have been back in London with her boys on 30 August, and not in Paris at all.

Nevertheless, Diana kept in touch with Marks by mobile phone, to find out how things were going with her and to fill Marks in with her own news as well. She called Marks from the French Riviera on 23 August, a week before her death. The conversation turned around to Diana's relationship with Dodi, and the Princess spelled out her thoughts. Marks recalls, 'Diana told me about her friendship with Dodi Fayed and said that it was so hard for her to sit at home that summer and "watch the four walls of Kensington Palace". Those were her exact words. And when she had this opportunity, this further invitation to go back to the south of France, she thought she would have a fun time.'

Thinking back to what she and Diana spoke about over the phone at that time, Marks says, 'Diana was not in love with Dodi Fayed. No! Diana told me that she had a lovely time with him. They could talk and she felt a warmth with him; he was nothing further than that. Diana was somebody who, if she permitted you to enter her life, was all embracing. She would throw her arms around you. She would hug and kiss you. She would be responsive, lovely and sweet and warm, so when the press would see her with Dodi who was a lovely gentleman, and they'd see her hugging him, or kissing him, or embracing him, they were convinced that this was it, when it really wasn't, and all she was doing was having a lovely summer and enjoying herself with a lovely gentleman.

'But she knew the summer was coming to an end and she'd told me she was looking forward to getting back to Kensington Palace; to being with her boys, and that she would then be on her own, moving on to the next charity that she was going to get involved with and that Dodi would be a past chapter of her life.'

While the world's press were pursuing Diana and Dodi round the Mediterranean, Diana was still maintaining her contact with the Khan family. This in itself is extremely revealing, given that Hasnat Khan had ended their relationship some time in late July. It suggests that she had not given up all hope of a reconciliation.

Professor Jawad Khan, the heart surgeon, and his family were still on holiday in Stratford-upon-Avon, and Diana had originally planned to come back and stay with them following her return from the south of France on 31 August.

She had been keeping in close contact with them about her holiday plans throughout the summer, even originally asking Jawad about taking his two youngest children with her and her own two boys when the holiday plans with Fayed's family had been finalized for July. Jawad had thought about it, but in the end said 'No'. Diana was accustomed to discussing the affairs of the heart with Jawad, often joking about what the press were saying about her.

Now Diana was on the telephone to Professor Jawad again, in what appeared to be an apologetic mood. Jawad cannot remember the exact date of the call, but says it was about a week before her death. What he is certain about is that it followed the appearance of the infamous 'KISS' picture, which he had seen. Referring to the picture, Jawad said to Diana, 'Are you trying to make Hasnat jealous? It's stupid, it won't work, it'll backfire!' Diana deflected the question, replying, 'There isn't anything in it.' She said, 'I've known [Dodi's] family for a long time, they were friends of my father, I've known Dodi for a long time as well; there's nothing in it. I'll see you next week, and we'll talk about it.'

Despite all the speculation of an engagement to Dodi in the newspapers, Diana wanted to reassure the Khan family that 'there was nothing in it'.

Diana repeated these thoughts to her close friend Roberto Devorik, who spoke to her on 28 August, only three days before her death. 'She called me from her mobile. I think she was near Portofino. I heard her voice, it sounded so positive, so strong. She told me, "I'm having a great time." I said, "Yes, I can see. What is all this kissing in front of the rest of the world? I leave you semi alone and I come back to organize this gala and now I see your great romance! Do you mean I have to call Christian Lacroix and ask him to make you a new wedding dress?" Diana said [in her usual way, she always used to say to me "Don't start" . . .], "Don't start, you're Latin, you should know what a summer romance is all about!" I knew Diana quite well, and if Mr Fayed hears me he would be disappointed and Dodi was a charming guy, but Diana would not take a decision in a month, or two months or three months to get married. It would have been a great surprise to all of us who knew her. A big big surprise.'

A couple of days earlier, Diana made her last call to Lady Elsa Bowker.

Lady Bowker was in her small private room watching television without any particular interest, when suddenly on the screen she saw Diana, pictured wearing her bathing suit; carrying a pair of slippers in one hand, and her mobile phone in the other. She was followed by Dodi.

Suddenly Lady Bowker heard the phone ringing, which upset her, because she didn't want to be disturbed. Nevertheless she answered it and heard a strong voice saying, 'Elsa.' Lady Bowker said, 'Who are you?' The voice said, 'How can you ask me who I am? I am Diana!' Lady Bowker asked her what she had done with her voice; she didn't recognize it because it sounded so different, so strong. Diana told her, 'It's strong because I am a very strong woman now; I fear nothing.' Bowker asked, 'Are you getting married?' and laughed and said to her, 'Shall I speak Arabic to you now, what do you think?' Diana laughed back and said, 'Elsa, I'm coming back, I'll come and see you Thursday [Diana had originally been scheduled to arrive back earlier] and talk to you then.' Lady Bowker says, 'I knew that it meant "No, I am not getting married; definitely not!" And I am positive she would have never married him because if that had been her intention she would have told me on the phone.'

Only the day before the crash, Lady Annabel Goldsmith spoke to Diana on the phone. Lady Annabel asked how things were going. Diana told her she was having a wonderful time, but that the last thing she needed was a new marriage.[1]

It could be argued that Diana would not rush to tell her friends about an engagement knowing that the majority of them would disapprove. It is possible that she might have been waiting to return to England before breaking the news to friends and family. However, if there had been any hint of approval from just one of those friends about Dodi, Diana would have told them her plans. It does not add up then that Roberto Devorik who thinks of Dodi as a 'charming guy' and Lana Marks who calls Dodi a lovely

1 *Sunday Telegraph*, 15 February 1998

gentleman were only told that she was enjoying a summer fling, and having a 'lovely time'. Nor does it make sense that she would be phoning the Khan family and telling them 'there was nothing in it' and planning to see them after her return from France if she had indeed been intending an engagement to Dodi.

So if she wasn't preparing to tie the marital knot with Dodi Fayed, what did Diana's friends think she was doing that last summer? It is the view of many of them – even though they weren't aware of the orchestration of the 'KISS' pictures – that by displaying her affection so overtly for Dodi she had been trying to make Hasnat jealous, to win him back and force him into making a commitment to her.

Imran Khan says he would be surprised if something as deep as she felt for Dr Hasnat could have been over so quickly. Only a few months earlier she had demonstrated such commitment to him while in Lahore. After all, Diana was involved with Hasnat Khan for two years and had spent a mere twenty-six days with Dodi. Lady Elsa Bowker says, 'I have the feeling – I can't confirm it – that the relationship with Dodi was to try to make Hasnat Khan jealous.'

It seems clear that from Diana's point of view she hoped there was still a future in her relationship with Hasnat. She was doing her best to make sure a senior member of the Khan family knew that her relationship with Dodi was not serious, and why do that if she wasn't still committed to Hasnat? There was surely enough momentum to suggest that it was too soon for her to be so totally smitten by somebody else, and for all thought of her two-year relationship and her attempts to marry into the Khan family to be so quickly and so easily forgotten.

Following Diana's arrival in the south of France to stay at the Fayed villa on 14 July, the events that were to follow took place at breakneck speed, and for somebody who was in a vulnerable position it could be all too easy to be swept up by it all. Fate has not given Diana the luxury of allowing the dust to settle, or the opportunity for calm reflection. For these reasons, the most that can reliably be said about those last twenty-six days with Dodi were that she enjoyed it for what it was. Another trusted friend expresses it thus. 'She loved being part of Dodi's family as she had wanted to be part of Hasnat's family too. But it is my belief she would have come back from her holiday with Dodi and gone back to Hasnat and he would have taken her back.'

24

The Rescue Mission

There is one final piece of the jigsaw that Diana was putting in place in that last summer which helps to clarify her actions and state of mind. It also adds terrible poignancy to the tragic way in which events were to unfold

What has not been known until now is that Diana had placed her hopes on one final attempt to win Hasnat back. Even while she shared intimate moments with Dodi in the south of France, the plan that had been formulated was beginning to take shape.

Before leaving Pakistan at the end of May 1997 she had a heart-to-heart chat with Imran Khan, at the end of her two-day trip to Lahore. This was during her stay at Imran and Jemima's house, after she had met with Hasnat Khan's family. On returning from the family meeting, she could only hope that she had made a good impression on them.

Sitting there with Imran, she spelled out her true feelings about Hasnat Khan. She told Imran she was desperate to make her relationship with Hasnat work. 'Princess Diana wanted to marry him, she really had decided *he was the man* she wanted to live with,' says Imran.

Diana told Imran that Hasnat Khan was proving difficult to convince. He did not want the publicity, he wanted to lead a private life. 'She kept saying he was very shy, and he didn't want to be in a marriage where there would be a media circus around all the time.'

While conveying her feelings to Imran Khan she admitted she felt close to no one. At the same time she relayed her sense of frustration because Hasnat appeared to be so noncommittal.

Hearing her talk in this way, Imran felt great sorrow for her. He says that she was just 'so sad' and 'so lonely'. Listening to just one side of the story he couldn't comprehend why Hasnat might be reluctant to commit himself. So he offered to act as a go-between and to talk to Hasnat Khan himself to try to move the relationship on.

The meeting was to be a friendly man-to-man chat in London, based on a sharing of understood feelings and problems. Imran had the experience of marrying outside his culture and felt that if there were issues that he could discuss, or if there was some advice he could give, then he might be able to help. At the very least he would be able to find out the real reason for the impasse, as there might have been something more behind Hasnat's obvious concerns that Diana was not aware of.

Acting on Diana's behalf then, Imran Khan was preparing for his mission on a planned trip to London over that last final summer. But before Khan was able to make the journey, news broke of the Paris crash. It was the final twist in a tale of terrible ironies. 'I was supposed to go to London, I had to go to London anyway, and before that could happen, unfortunately that tragic incident took place,' says Khan.

25

Her Last Love

Most of those who knew Diana well believe that Hasnat Khan had been a much more serious relationship to her than Dodi ever could have been. She had invested a huge amount of time and emotion in getting to know the doctor's family, and in coming to terms with how she could handle a move abroad or a liaison with a different culture. Imran Khan attests to Diana's love and keen wish to marry Hasnat; she had spoken to Professor Christian Barnard of her desire to have his children.

Hasnat Khan in turn truly loved Diana, and he wanted to marry her. The problem for him was that she was the Princess of Wales. One of the things he loved most about her was not her title or her status, but the fact she had such empathy with the patients he was treating. She was someone who shared his passion for caring for the sick. In the end the gulf between them was too great for Khan to bridge in his own mind, but this had less to do with religion or culture, but more to do with Diana's 'baggage'. Although Khan's mother may have been seen as the key factor that influenced the demise of the relationship, in the final analysis she was only a small part of the equation. Khan is thoroughly westernized now, but more crucially he has already shown his parents he will not marry against his will.

Although Hasnat Khan had ended their relationship just

before the first holiday with Dodi, many of her friends believe Diana would have tried to make him change his mind. She had gone out of her way to prove to him she could 'fit in', and believed, perhaps somewhat naïvely, that a move abroad would mean the press attention would be less intense. Certainly Diana was planning to spend more time with Hasnat Khan's family in Stratford-upon-Avon.

Having failed to persuade him that a life together could work out, she had resorted to dramatic measures in a last desperate attempt to provoke a reaction from him. In part her strategy may have worked. Although Khan gave an interview to the press after the 'KISS' pictures appeared, wishing Diana and Dodi well, it seems clear he would have felt acute anguish on seeing the pictures, and he could not have lost his love for Diana that easily. In all probability he guessed what Diana was up to, he knew she was deliberately being pictured with Dodi in order to send him a message – 'Look at me, I am enjoying myself without you' – a message she hoped would strike his heart and make him jealous. Had Diana not gone to Paris, and gone back to London instead, then Imran Khan would have met with Hasnat and tried to talk him round. If that had happened who knows how things would have turned out in the end? The story of Diana and Hasnat Khan is ultimately tragic because they were so in love, and yet unable through circumstances to be together. Just four weeks after he had called the relationship off, Khan's pain at hearing of Diana's death is unimaginable.

Had her relationship with Khan recommenced, and had it grown, then it could have had tremendous international significance. Professor Akbar Ahmed of Cambridge University, who has since been appointed Pakistan's ambassador to London, believes Diana would have created greater understanding between Christianity and Islam, and been a bridge between Europe and Asia, colour and race. 'Diana was an example of someone prepared to break all the barriers. She had unique qualities that would have equipped her to be an ambassador between the East and the West. Her Royal position gave her a kind of aura, and she had great physical presence, warmth, beauty and charm. She lacked cynicism or suspicion, and had the good faith to become part of a different culture. She was breaking all the barriers and going down to the poorest people. She really captured the imagination as no one else could.'

Ahmed accepts that some people would contradict him, by pointing out that Diana got divorced, she had affairs, and some Muslims say she was a 'woman of easy virtue', but Ahmed feels her compassion transcended the other shortcomings. 'That is what she had and that is what makes her spiritual, not in the Orthodox way that she is religious in a traditional sense but in the sense of compassion.'

The idea of having a relationship just because the world expected great things of you would not have been an attraction for Hasnat Khan, rather the reverse would have been the case. Diana also did not aspire to the lofty heights that others might have aspired to for her had she indeed married a Muslim. Diana was mostly interested in the East as a possible answer to her own quest for inner peace, for stability, affection, love and meaning. She turned to Muslims because they embraced a way of thinking that held deep resonance for her.

Would Diana ultimately have married a Muslim? Diana's friends have widely differing opinions about what might have happened. Some believe that Hasnat Khan was right for Diana at the time, but that her journey East was only a stage in her life; it would not have been the conclusion of her quest. Others believe she pursued Khan most of all because he remained always just beyond reach, but actually she would never have married a Muslim. Others still believe that she and Hasnat would have got back together and stayed together. We just cannot know.

One thing, however, seems certain; Khan did not like the limelight or attendant press that accompanied Diana wherever she went. Diana, on the other hand, despite loathing the invasion of her privacy, had a preoccupation with her own image and celebrity, and the glamorous mystique she enjoyed would have disappeared had she moved to some backwater with Khan to pursue a life of quiet dedication. Such a life could not have suited Diana; she needed to see her own image in the press in order to believe in who she was, and ultimately to justify her own existence.

Once she and her friend Roberto Devorik were talking and he asked her, 'Diana, do you think one day you are really going to be happy?' And she replied, 'Roberto, perhaps God put me in this world with a duty not of me being happy, but of making other people happy.' Diana made this comment at the age of thirty-one. By the time of her death she had found the ability to make other people happy, but she was also learning to be happy herself.

Her relationship both with Khan and with his family coincided with her discovery that she was able to campaign effectively on the world stage and not just be seen as a photogenic princess, and she was emerging as a much stronger woman. Her friends had noticed a change in her. Both Roberto Devorik and Lady Bowker comment on how Diana's voice had grown stronger over the final summer, and Diana herself said she was a strong person now. Her childhood fears of being abandoned, worthless and unloved were certainly not gone, but they were diminished, and she was on the road to finally being at peace with herself.

When Diana travelled to Bosnia, she was looking wonderful and she was physically strong, too. She had taken no secretaries, ladies in waiting or entourage. She had Paul Burrell to do her hair, and she did her own make-up. She was wearing jeans and shirts, and seemed happy with her own appearance, at the same time as she was in the public eye. Her search for love had transformed from a personal search to a wider compassion that she wanted to share with the world. She had gained a degree of emotional and mental confidence, and for the first time was able to face the future with an independent mind.

Her maturing was reflected in her relations with Prince Charles. They had become less strained; she had learned how to love Charles as a friend and as an adult. When Sir Laurens

Van der Post, Prince Charles's mentor, died in 1996, Diana wrote a carefully worded letter of heartfelt sympathy saying that she of all people knew how it felt to lose somebody that close. Charles didn't reply in the normal way with another letter, but called Diana personally to thank her for her understanding. It opened the door wider to a dialogue that was to continue until the end, and there was an undoubted softening between them and a new warmth.

Even much of Diana's old resentment about Camilla Parker Bowles seemed to have diminished. Since Hasnat Khan was the first person who Diana felt had loved her for herself, the Princess had finally come to appreciate and understand what true love was.

Lady Bowker tells of one conversation in the final few weeks of Diana's life. 'It was the first time she told me something really funny. She told me, "Elsa, you know what I thought the other day? It was Camilla's birthday and Charles was giving the party at Highgrove. What a wonderful idea if I were to put on my bathing suit and hide under the birthday cake and suddenly just jump out!" And she told me, "I respect the love she has for Charles because I know what love is now." I don't know how she knew it, but I think it is because of Dr Hasnat Khan.'

It was the greatest gift he ever gave her.

26

The Funeral

Hasnat Khan was at home sleeping in his London flat when the phone rang on the morning of 31 August. His family in Pakistan had already heard the news, as they were several hours ahead. Immediately they heard they picked up the phone to London. It was his mother who reacted first and actually broke the news to Hasnat. For a while he didn't believe it and sat numb, hardly taking it in.

Hasnat was not the only member of the Khan family to feel distraught. For a long time the rest of the family didn't know how to break the news to Appa, and they avoided doing so for several hours. Eventually they reached a point where they could conceal it no longer, and suddenly, according to the family, 'All hell broke loose in that house.'

'Why did this happen?' the old lady demanded.

Her question was echoed around the world as a profound sense of shock swept across the globe from Sydney to Calcutta, from Paris to Cape Town.

News of Diana's death seemed impossible to absorb. People were moved beyond words; the tragedy shattered all thoughts of normal activity.

At the time of the crash, Imran Khan happened to be in a very remote part of Pakistan, where the villages don't have electricity, and so the only connection to the outside world is by radio.

He was touring that part of the country when someone told him that the village women had heard there had been a terrible accident, and then it was confirmed that Diana was dead. Khan says everyone in the village gathered together as if someone very close to them had died; there was just a deep, shared sense of sadness.

'In Islam death is not taken the same way as in the West. In Islam it is believed that death is the will of God, and therefore there's a much greater acceptance. But in Diana's case the air hung with depression; no one talked, the function I was attending just disintegrated,' says Khan.

Lady Bowker received a phone call from Roberto Devorik in the early hours of the morning, telling her there had been an accident, and Simone Simmons was in bed when she woke with a jolt and switched the television on. Fumbling to find her contact lenses, she listened to the news of Diana's death with deep shock.

Friends of the Princess say it was like being in a Dalí painting; everything felt very surreal.

The outpourings of grief were public, on the streets and not just behind closed doors. The displays of sorrow demonstrated in huge measure the affection felt for Diana. In London, capital of a nation normally reserved in its emotions, people were queuing ten deep along the entire length of The Mall for more than six hours at a time to sign condolence books at St James's Palace.

On the day of the funeral, the quietness of the streets up and down Britain suggested that hundreds of thousands of shoppers had chosen to stay in and watch television. Those who had gone to work found excuses and gravitated towards the nearest screen. Everyone felt they knew her; everyone shared in the tragedy.

In London there were hysterical scenes as the funeral cortège left Kensington Palace on its way to Westminster Abbey.

In Paris, awe at the spectacle of her funeral was mingled with guilt.

In Bosnia, victims of landmines watched in tears as the funeral procession made its slow way through London.

In India, there were unusual scenes of deserted streets as millions of people, already mourning the death of Mother Teresa, returned home to grieve privately.

In Australia, St Andrew's Cathedral in Sydney and churches nationwide held special memorial services attended by thousands.

The world had lost an icon, a figurehead, someone everyone somehow felt they could identify with. A myth had been born out of the life and death of a woman perceived to be extraordinary but who in truth only ever yearned to be loved.

For those close to her the grief was different; it was an intimate personal mourning on the one hand, yet they were aware that the entire world was there to share in it.

Close friends of Diana took their numbered seats in Westminster Abbey along with the other 2000 people who were there that morning. Lady Bowker was so distressed at Diana's death she couldn't face going to the service and had taken to her bed. In Lahore the family gathered round the television set, and in Hendon, Simone Simmons sat with her friend Ursula.

But for one man the death of Diana was more painful and more devastating than can possibly ever be imagined. And no one except those closest to him knew of his grief and anguish.

On 6 September 1997, while the world's media focused on more high-profile celebrities, Hasnat Khan sat quietly devastated and unnoticed in the middle of a row of pews at Westminster Abbey. He was wearing a pair of dark sunglasses that had been a gift from Diana. Sitting next to him was his aunt, Jane Khan. Their tickets had been organized by Paul Burrell.

As the soprano Lynne Dawson sang from Diana's favourite, the Verdi Requiem, pleading to God to bring the dead eternal rest, and to let perpetual light shine upon them, Hasnat's head dropped forward – private to the end.

EPILOGUE

To this day Hasnat Khan still works at the Royal Brompton Hospital, where he devotes his life to saving the lives of others.

His uncle, Ashfaq Ahmed, believes he will go on to be a successful heart surgeon, get married, and have a family, but that he will never recover from his tragic loss.

On that May evening in Lahore when Diana visited the Model Town house to meet the Khan family, a roll of film was taken. The idea was that Hasnat should see the photographs, and so a few weeks later the family sent him the roll of film by post.

To this day it remains in a drawer. The photos have never been developed.

Appendix 1: Timeline

1961

July 1   Diana born, at Park House, on the Queen's Sandringham Estate in Norfolk

Aug 30   Diana christened

1967

Summer: Diana's parents decide on a trial separation

Sep   The marriage finally collapses. Diana's mother, Frances, initially takes the children with her

Dec   Diana's father announces that he has enrolled the children in local schools. Therefore they will now remain at Park House

1969

May 2   Diana's mother, Frances, marries Peter Shand Kydd

1971

Feb   Mary Clarke appointed as Diana's nanny

1972   Diana's mother and her new husband move to the remote Isle of Seil, off the west coast of Scotland

1978

Sept   Diana's father, Earl Spencer, collapses after a massive brain haemorrhage

Nov	Earl Spencer is moved to the Royal Brompton Hospital, where Diana meets Professor Jawad Khan for the first time
1981 **Feb 6**	Prince Charles proposes to Lady Diana Spencer in the nursery of Windsor Castle
Jul 29	The wedding of Prince Charles and Diana at St Paul's Cathedral
1982 **Jun 21**	Birth of Prince William
1984 **Sep 15**	Birth of Prince Harry
1986 **Jul**	Diana first meets Dodi Fayed at a polo match.
1990 **Jun 27**	Diana's private secretary writes to the Royal Anthropological Society asking for a briefing on Pakistan
Sep 13	Prof Akbar Ahmed gives a lecture to Diana at the Royal Anthropological Society
1991 **Sep 16**	Prof Ahmed invited to tea at Kensington Palace, where he gives Diana advice for her forthcoming solo visit to Pakistan
Sep 22	Diana's five-day visit to Pakistan begins
Sep 26	Diana visits Lahore's King Edward Medical College, where she is introduced again to Professor Jawad Khan

1992
Feb 10 Prince Charles and Princess Diana arrive in India at the start of a six-day official visit

Feb 11 Diana poses alone for photographers in front of the Taj Mahal

Feb 12 Polo match in Jaipur, at which the cameras capture Diana turning her head away just as her husband is about to kiss her

The Indian visit ends with Charles going to a private engagement in Nepal, while Diana visits Mother Teresa's Missionaries of Charity

Mar 29 Diana's father, Earl Spencer, dies of a heart attack. Diana is on a skiing holiday in Austria with Charles when she receives the news

Jun 16 Publication of Andrew Morton's book, *Diana, Her True Story*

Dec 9 Charles and Diana agree to separate

1993
Nov Oliver Hoare brings Diana to meet Lady Elsa Bowker, who had known her when she was a teenager

Dec Diana meets Simone Simmons

1994
Apr Diana photographed on an Austrian ski chalet balcony, reading *Discovering Islam* by Prof Akbar Ahmed

1995
Sep 1 Hasnat Khan is introduced to Diana at the Royal Brompton Hospital in London

Sep 1–18 Diana visits Joseph Toffolo at the Royal Brompton and gets to know Khan. He acts as her willing guide around the hospital

Nov 20	*Panorama* interview with Martin Bashir transmitted
Nov 30	Diana spotted by a *News of the World* photographer, leaving the Royal Brompton Hospital late at night
Dec 12	British Prime Minister John Major announces Charles and Diana's formal separation
Dec 18	Diana receives the Queen's handwritten request for a divorce from Charles
Dec 25	Diana spends Christmas Day alone at Kensington Palace

1996

Feb 20	Diana arrives in Pakistan for a two-day visit, at the invitation of Imran and Jemima Khan
Feb 21	Diana tours Imran Khan's Shaukat Khanum Memorial Cancer Hospital, where she meets seven-year-old Ashraf Mohammed
Apr 23	Diana watches heart operation at Harefield Hospital filmed by Sky TV
Jul 4	Prince Charles's lawyers announce the divorce settlement. Diana is wearing the Pakistani outfit designed by Rizwan Beyg. In the evening she attends a dinner at the Dorchester Hotel in London to raise money for Imran Khan's hospital
Jul 12	Final agreement of the divorce settlement
Jul 15	Charles and Diana file their 'decree nisi' Diana invites Appa, Omar and Jane for tea at Kensington Palace
Aug 28	Finalization of the divorce from Charles She tells her close circle of friends of her plans to remarry now she is free of the House of Windsor
Oct 13	Diana flies to Italian resort of Rimini to accept a humanitarian award. While there she befriends South

African heart surgeon, Prof. Christian Barnard, another award recipient

Oct 31   Diana flies to Sydney

Nov 1   Diana officially opens the Victor Chang Institute

Nov 3   *Sunday Mirror* newspaper headlines 'Di's new love – How Princess Di fell in love with Hasnat Khan'

Nov 4   *Daily Mail* article written by Richard Kay describes the previous day's report as 'bullshit'

1997

Jan 14   Diana meets child victims of landmines in an Angolan hospital

Jan 15   Diana makes her famous walk through an Angolan minefield

May 22   Diana arrives in Pakistan again, staying at the house of Imran and Jemima Khan
On the same day, British Foreign Secretary Robin Cook declares a complete ban on British trade in landmines
During her stay she drives with Imran's sisters to the Model Town home of Hasnat Khan's family. There she tries to impress Hasnat's mother. Later that night Imran volunteers to act as her go-between with Hasnat

Jun 6   Diana spotted nightclubbing with Gulu Lalvani, who invites her to Thailand

Jun 11   Diana accepts Mohamed Fayed's holiday invitation to the south of France

Jun 21   Diana spends the entire day with visiting members of Hasnat Khan's family, including Nanny Appa, at the Stratford home of Omar and Jane. Diana takes the children to Tesco supermarket, pretending to be 'Sharon'

Jun 25 Christie's in New York raises over two million pounds by auctioning seventy-nine of Diana's dresses. The money goes to charity

Jul 1 Diana's thirty-sixth birthday

Jul 11 Beginning of Diana's holiday with her two sons at the Fayed villa in St Tropez

Jul 14 Diana, fed up with press attention, gives an impromptu news conference at sea, during which she promises, 'You will get a big surprise with the next thing I do'
On the same day, Dodi Fayed arrives on board the *Jonikal*, after being summoned by his father

Jul 15 Diana's friend, fashion designer Gianni Versace, is murdered

Jul 16 Hasnat advised by a confidant to call the relationship off

Jul 18 Newspapers full of photographs of Diana swimming, diving and jet-skiing. It is also the day of Camilla Parker Bowles's 50th birthday party at Highgrove House

Jul 19 Sir James Goldsmith, father of Jemima Khan, dies
At some point during the holiday Diana phones Hasnat Khan's Chelsea flat. His uncle picks up the phone and she asks him to tell Hasnat to ring her when she gets back

Jul 20 Diana and the princes fly back to London

Jul 22 Diana attends funeral service in Milan for Gianni Versace
Hasnat Khan breaks off relationship with Diana

Jul 24 Lana Marks's father dies, and she has to call off the holiday she had been planning with Diana in August

Jul 26 Diana flies to Paris for hastily arranged 'date' with Dodi Fayed

Jul 27	Diana returns to London
Jul 30	Photographer Jason Fraser is tipped off about Diana and Dodi's impending cruise on the *Jonikal*
Jul 31	Diana joins Dodi again for another cruise aboard the *Jonikal*
Aug 2	Italian photographer Mario Brenna, alerted by Jason Fraser, awaits the right moment to take photographs of Diana and Dodi
Aug 4	Brenna takes the infamous 'KISS' pictures
Aug 8	Diana flies to Bosnia to continue her landmines campaign
Aug 10	The *Sunday Mirror* publishes the 'KISS' picture, and everyone is talking of a romance between Diana and Dodi
Aug 11	Diana returns from Bosnia. The 'KISS' pictures don't trouble her
Aug 21	Diana flies out with Dodi to Nice. Jason Fraser is waiting on the quayside at St Laurent-du-Var
Aug 23	Diana calls Lana Marks, saying she was looking forward to returning home, and that Dodi would soon be 'a past chapter' in her life
Aug 25	Diana calls Jason Fraser and asks why the previous day's photographs had been so grainy. She also calls Lady Elsa Bowker, who understood from the conversation that Diana had no plans to get married to Dodi
Aug 26	Diana calls Prof Jawad Khan, who tells her that if she is trying to make Hasnat jealous with the 'KISS' pictures, it won't work. She tells him there's nothing in her relationship with Dodi
Aug 28	Diana calls Roberto Devorik, telling Devorik that the affair with Dodi is just a 'summer romance'

Aug 30   Diana speaks to Lady Annabel Goldsmith on the phone, and says she needs a new marriage like a bad rash on her face

Aug 31   In the early hours of the morning, the car carrying Diana and Dodi crashes, killing both of them

Sep 6   Diana's funeral

Appendix 2: Sources

The sources for this book were interviews, private letters and, to a lesser extent, newspaper reports, magazine articles and books.

Thirty-nine first-hand witnesses were interviewed in the research for the book. Fourteen of those who provided crucial testimony preferred to remain anonymous although their key contributions have added greatly to the book. Countless others confirmed or corrected points of fact.

Thank you to: Professor Akbar Ahmed, Ashfaq Ahmed, Maulana Abdul Qadir Azad, Rizwan Beyg, Lady Elsa Bowker, Sister Christie, Mary Clarke, Roberto Devorik, Sandra Erikson, Debbie Frank, Abida Hussain, Aleema Khan, 'Nanny' Appa Khan, Imran Khan, Professor Jawad Khan, Maryam Khan, Salahuddin Khan, Uzma Khan, Sunita Kumar, Lana Marks, Jugnu Mohsin, Simone Simmons, Penny Thornton, Oonagh Toffolo, Mike Whitlam.

Thank you to Jonathan Benthall for providing relevant documentation concerning the visit to the Royal Anthropological Institute in September 1990 by the Princess of Wales.

The following books were referred to:

Bower, Tom

Fayed: The Unauthorized Biography (Macmillan Publishers Ltd, 1998)

Campbell, Lady Colin

Diana in Private (Smith Gryphon Limited, 1992)

Clarke, Mary — *Little Girl Lost* (A Birch Lane Press Book, 1996)

Delorm, Rene
with Barry Fox and Nadine Taylor — *Diana and Dodi: A Love Story* (Pocket Books, 1998)

Junor, Penny — *Charles, Victim or Villain?* (Harper-Collins, 1998)

MacArthur, Brian, ed. — *Requiem: Diana Princess of Wales 1961 – 1997: Memories and Tributes* (Pavilion Books Ltd. 1997)

Morton, Andrew — *Diana, Her True Story – In Her Own Words* (Michael O'Mara, 1997)

Pasternak, Anna — *Princess in Love* (Bloomsbury Publishing Plc, 1994)

Simmons, Simone
with Susan Hill — *Diana: The Secret Years* (Michael O'Mara 1998)

Thornton, Penny — *With Love from Diana* (Pocket Books, 1995)

Appendix 3: List of Illustrations

Pictures are listed by source. Page numbers refer to the plate sections.

Acknowledgements

This book originated with a TV documentary about Diana, and I would like to thank London Weekend Television for allowing me access to the transcripts of interviews from that documentary. In particular Will Smith, deputy controller of factual programmes at LWT, has been a constant and valuable support, both in his dogged determination to see the film aired, and his eagerness and encouragement to see the book written.

Nisar Malik, a TV producer from Pakistan now based in London, accompanied me on my two trips to Pakistan. His authoritative and brilliant diplomacy, insightful assessments, and phlegmatic and imperturbable disposition during pivotal moments have without doubt greatly contributed to the depth of this book.

Meticulous sifting of relevant news articles, and efficient dispatch of poignant information, frequently outside office hours, by Fiona Sanson from LWT's research department was an invaluable constant during long winter months of solitude, and my dear friend Annie Venables slotted in research around her busy TV life in Melbourne to check out elements of the story in Sydney, Australia.

I must particularly thank Susanna Wadeson, Head of Books at Granada Media, for commissioning me to write this book in the first place, and for constantly championing my efforts to pursue journalistic enquiries in uncharted territory. Latterly my editor at Andre Deutsch, Ingrid Connell, has brought renewed warmth, wit, vigour and clever judgement to the project.

The bedrock of research on which the book is based was initially conducted by my team on the LWT film. Chief amongst those was Petra Coveney, whose first-class communication skills, sharp perceptions, tireless efforts in Pakistan, not to mention her journalistic excellence, under-

pinned the success of the documentary. Diensen Pamben brought with him a vitality and youthful energy that led to a spirited enquiry in Calcutta, and his natural affinity with all things visual was at the same time refreshing and reassuring. My cameraman Jonathon Harrison's zeal and commitment to the programme meant he often worked in his own time to devise ways of achieving visual and technical brilliance, and my film editor John Lee likewise often toiled selflessly in his own time to lend grace and beauty to the film; his incisive comments and weight of experience undoubtedly enhanced the richness of the finished product. Josephine Cocking and Marnie Sirota planned our logistics with military precision, and guaranteed the film's smooth passage through its various stages.

At the outset, Mike Brennan, senior producer at LWT, Stuart Higgins, Richard Kay and Andrew Morton all gave generously of their time, each drawing on their invaluable experience to provide me with advice and general background on Diana. I am very grateful to all of them.

I have already thanked the Khan family for accepting me into their midst during my research, but I also need to express my heartfelt gratitude for their boundless hospitality and warmth. On many occasions Yousef Salahuddin provided myself and members of my team with the most wonderful food, and unquestioned generosity in the surroundings of his magical havelli in Old Lahore, and Salman and Batool Batalvi offered not only their home and hospitality, but also their advice and friendship, and I thank them for the many evenings we spent enveloped in affectionate discussion.

Finally, I cannot thank the contributors to this book enough for all their patience, dedication and encouragement throughout the last year; theirs are all contributions I shall never forget.

Last, but by no means least, my dearest husband Mark has been a constant companion and sounding board whether over breakfast, dinner, the phone, by email, toiling up mountainsides in the Lakes, or increasingly long cycle rides along the Thames. His invaluable and pertinent thoughts have helped to shape parts of the book, and often brought a clarity and sharpness all of their own. It is true to say that without his belief in me, and unwavering support of my efforts, this book would not have been written; so for your remarkable and singular contribution, Mark, thank you.

Index